S. Hrg. 114–216

SUPPORTING THE WARFIGHTER OF TODAY AND TOMORROW

HEARING

BEFORE THE

COMMITTEE ON ARMED SERVICES
UNITED STATES SENATE

ONE HUNDRED FOURTEENTH CONGRESS

FIRST SESSION

DECEMBER 3, 2015

Printed for the use of the Committee on Armed Services

Available via the World Wide Web: http://www.fdsys.gov/

U.S. GOVERNMENT PUBLISHING OFFICE

99–664 PDF   WASHINGTON : 2016

For sale by the Superintendent of Documents, U.S. Government Publishing Office
Internet: bookstore.gpo.gov   Phone: toll free (866) 512–1800; DC area (202) 512–1800
Fax: (202) 512–2104   Mail: Stop IDCC, Washington, DC 20402–0001

(II)

CONTENTS

DECEMBER 3, 2015

(III)

SUPPORTING THE WARFIGHTER OF TODAY AND TOMORROW

THURSDAY, DECEMBER 3, 2015

U.S. SENATE
COMMITTEE ON ARMED SERVICES
Washington, D.C.

The committee met, pursuant to notice, at 9:31 a.m. in Room SD–106, Dirksen Senate Office Building, Senator John McCain (chairman) presiding.

Committee Members Present: Senators McCain, Ayotte, Fischer, Ernst, Tillis, Sullivan, Reed, McCaskill, Manchin, Gillibrand, Donnelly, Hirono, and King.

OPENING STATEMENT OF SENATOR JOHN McCAIN, CHAIRMAN

Chairman McCAIN. The Senate Armed Services Committee meets to continue our series of hearings on defense reform. In our three previous hearings, we have reviewed the effects of the Goldwater-Nichols reforms on our defense acquisition, management, and personnel systems. In today's hearings and the two that will follow it, we will consider what most view as the essence of Goldwater-Nichols: the roles and responsibilities of the Secretary of Defense, the Chairman of the Joint Chiefs of Staff, the service secretaries and service chiefs, and the combatant commanders. This morning we seek to understand whether these civilian and military leadership organizations can function better to support the warfighters of today and tomorrow.

We are fortunate to welcome a distinguished panel of witnesses who have grappled with these challenging issues over their many years of service to our Nation: the Honorable Michael B. Donley, former Secretary of the Air Force; Lieutenant General Michael T. Flynn, former Director of the Defense Intelligence Agency; and General James Jones, former National Security Advisor; Supreme Allied Commander and Commander of U.S. European Command; and Commandant of the Marine Corps. We welcome you this morning.

30 years ago, Congress passed Goldwater-Nichols in response to serious concerns about the effectiveness of our military. The failure of the Iranian hostage rescue mission in 1980 and poor coordination between the services during the invasion of Grenada in 1983 were clear signs that something was wrong. Congress and others concluded that these failures were driven by a number of factors, including the absence of unity of command and an inability to operate jointly.

Goldwater-Nichols sought to address these problems by making the unified commanders explicitly responsible to the President and the Secretary of Defense for the performance of missions and preparedness of their commands. Combatant commanders were given the ability to issue authoritative direction on all aspects of operations, joint training, logistics, internal chains of command, and personnel within their assigned areas of responsibility. Goldwater-Nichols also removed the Joint Chiefs of Staff from the operational chain of command and prevented the services from moving forces in and out of regional commands without approval.

Just 5 years after the passage of Goldwater-Nichols, America's rapid and stunning victory in the 1991 Gulf War seemed to suggest that these reforms had worked. However, more recent experience on the battlefield has led to renewed concern about the respective roles and responsibilities of the service chiefs and the combatant commanders as conceived in Goldwater-Nichols.

A decade and a half of war in Afghanistan and Iraq suggests that the Department of Defense is not optimally organized for protracted conflicts. As Secretary Gates recently testified to this committee, his experience as a wartime secretary led him to conclude that the Department of Defense is, quote, designed to plan for war but not to wage war, at least for the long term. Indeed, whatever one thinks about the circumstances by which we all went to war in Iraq 12 years ago, it should be deeply concerning to all of us that our Nation was losing that war for 3 years, and the strategy that ultimately turned things around did not emerge from the system, but rather from a small group of internal insurgents and outside experts working around the system. That is a compelling indictment of our defense organization.

For some, including Secretary Gates, Goldwater-Nichols succeeded all too well by turning the services into force providers that are perhaps too walled off from operational responsibilities. With a confined focus on the train and equip mission, the services have overwhelmingly concentrated more on delivering long-term programs of record than urgently needed capabilities in current conflicts.

While this problem raises serious questions, we must be cautious of the other extreme. If combatant commanders were fully resourced with everything they believe is necessary for their theater, the Department of Defense would be totally sapped of resources to invest in critical technologies needed to counter future adversaries. I look forward to our witnesses' views on whether the Department could strike a better balance between supporting both the warfighters of today and tomorrow and if so, how.

At the same time, we must also ensure that the operational organization of our military accurately reflects and responds to our present and future national security challenges. Our Nation confronts the most diverse and complex array of crises since the end of World War II, from ISIL [the Islamic State of Iraq and the Levant] and Al Qaeda, to North Korea and Iran, to Russia and China. What all of these threats have in common is that they are not confined to a single region of the world. They span multiple regions and domains of military activities. Our combatant commands are still predominantly geographically. We must ensure that our defense organization has the regional and functional flexibility and agility to address cross-cutting national security missions.

Many of our prior witnesses have observed that combatant commands no longer directly fight wars, as Goldwater-Nichols originally envisioned. Instead, that is done by joint task forces established on an ad hoc basis and tailored to a given contingency operation. This makes the dramatic growth of the headquarters staffs at the combatant commands all the more difficult to justify. I would be eager to hear from our witnesses whether, 30 years after Goldwater-Nichols, we should consider re-imagining, reorganizing, or consolidating our combatant commands.

I thank our witnesses and look forward to their testimony.

Senator Reed?

STATEMENT OF SENATOR JACK REED

Senator REED. Well, thank you very much, Mr. Chairman. Let me join you in thanking the witnesses for not only being here today but for their extraordinary service to the Nation.

We have been holding a series of hearings that looks at the organization and processes of the Department of Defense, and the whole focus is to provide the best possible support for our warfighters. You gentlemen know more about that than practically anybody else. So thank you for joining us today.

A constant theme that has emerged in testimony from previous hearings is that the Department of Defense has a 20th century organization facing 21st century challenges: globalization, rapid adoption of new technology and particularly cyber, free flow of information. These are developments that have complicated the security environment by facilitating a rise of near-peer competitors and irregular threats from transnational terrorist groups. However, I believe these trends also provide opportunities to improve U.S. military capabilities which will support the warfighter if they can be effectively harnessed through updated organizational structures and processes. As yesterday's hearing made clear, the men and women who make up the all-volunteer force remain this committee's top concern. We must ensure they have the resources they need to complete their mission and return safely home.

Testifying on these issues earlier this fall—and I will again like the chairman quote Secretary Gates—he described the challenges he faced in delivering rapidly needed capabilities to troops in the field. He indicated that 'the only way I could get significant new or additional equipment to commanders in the field in weeks or months—not years—was to take control of the problem myself through special task forces and ad hoc processes.' He pointed out the MRAP [Mine-Resistant Ambush Protected Vehicle] as an example of one of those situations.

But he also pointed out that relying on this 'intense personal involvement' by the Secretary of Defense just does not work. There is not enough time in the day. So we have to, I think, together with the Department of Defense create structural changes that enable this rapid deployment and rapid support of our troops in the field. That is where your advice comes in very critically.

Goldwater-Nichols was enacted more than 30 years ago, and the Department continues to face difficulties to provide for the warfighter. That again is the essence of what we are all here to do, provide a process, an organizational structure, and a culture that delivers the support to the troops they need to protect the country.

Again, let me thank you, gentlemen, not only for your testimony but for your service.

Thank you, Mr. Chairman.

Chairman MCCAIN. I thank the witnesses and we will begin with you, Secretary Donley.

STATEMENT OF SECRETARY MICHAEL B. DONLEY, FORMER SECRETARY OF THE AIR FORCE

Mr. DONLEY. Thank you, Mr. Chairman and Ranking Member Reed, for holding this series of hearings. It has been a little over 30 years since I left this committee as a professional staff member and it is great to back.

While I was here, I did have any opportunity to work on Goldwater-Nichols and then, following my service here, went to the National Security Council where I also worked on these issues. So they are of special interest to me.

The hearings that the committee held in the mid- 1980s on Goldwater-Nichols were extremely formative in my career in educating me and I think other staff members of the committee on the operation of the Department of Defense. It stuck with me all these years. It has been of great benefit. I hope that one result of this great series of hearings that you have kicked off is that it will stimulate a deeper understanding of how our defense organization works.

My testimony today—by the way, this is a great panel to be part of, and I am honored to be here with General Flynn and longtime friend, General Jones, who I think when I was here before we referred to as Major Jones. It was Captain McCain. That goes way back, Mr. Chairman.

Chairman MCCAIN. He was much more pleasant in those days.

[Laughter.]

Mr. DONLEY. My testimony today is focused on the roles and relationships between the military departments and combatant commands and how and where these components interact to produce warfighting capabilities. I offer six recommendations for reducing resource-intensive military department and combatant command headquarters and better preparing joint and service headquarters for the demanding 21st century environment that you described, Mr. Chairman.

The context for my recommendations is section 346 of the justsigned fiscal year 2016 National Defense Authorization Act in which the committees require DOD [Department of Defense] to report on planned reductions to its major headquarters activities by March of next year.

The services interact with combatant commands in many ways on many levels to support joint operations. I would highlight two, command relationships and resource allocation, as representative of how services and COCOMs [combatant commands] interact to support warfighters of today and tomorrow.

Command relationships are at the intersection of how combatant commands choose to organize their subordinate commands and how services internally organize and present forces. In general, regional combatant commands choose to organize forces in land, maritime, and air domains within their assigned area, but both the regional and functional combatant commands also task organize with sub-unified commands or task forces for subregions, specific missions, or functions.

The services, of course, have major commands and subordinate commands such as numbered air forces, fleets, corps, armies, which are dual-hatted as components of the combatant commands. The services need to create internal command arrangements that satisfy both efficiency in their administrative command and organize train and equip responsibilities and effectiveness in their presentation of forces and in satisfying the operational command requirements as defined by nine combatant commanders. This intersection between the command relationships of four services and nine combatant commands is critical to the proper alignment of service forces under a unified command and it is directly pertinent to congressional and DOD interests in improving the efficiency of DOD's major headquarters.

So my first recommendation is that DOD and Congress review the service and combatant command relationships, but there are four important caveats here.

First, we should avoid generalizations. These command relationships are unique to each service and each combatant command.

Second, we probably should not assume that complex command arrangements reflect duplicative or unnecessary staff. You have to look. Dual-hatting, even triple-hatting where allied forces might be involved, makes good sense.

Also, we should not assume that opportunities for major savings might result. We need to review and take stock of previously harvested savings and efficiencies that have been taken by the services over the past several years.

I do have a predilection that Congress should not legislate command relationships at this level.

In resource allocation, executing roughly 80 percent of DOD resources, the services have to balance the size and capacity of their forces across multiple combat elements with the readiness of today's forces and investment in future capabilities. Combatant commands express their needs through multiple channels in the planning, programming, budgeting, and execution system, which is DOD's primary resource allocation process. These include their service components, integrated priority lists, and through the integrating role of the Chairman of the Joint Chiefs of Staff and the Joint Staff J–8 and the Joint Requirements Council. These responsibilities and organizational relationships established in DOD's key management processes ensure there is joint input and review in service resource allocation and acquisition. They provide combatant commands the necessary link and voice, but they are also intended to keep combatant commands focused on their deterrence, warfighting, planning, and engagement responsibilities minimizing the need for combatant command headquarters to have large programming staffs duplicating the work of their service force providers.

At the same time, the combatant commands need J–8 functions to interact with the joint staff and the services on matters related to program evaluation and resource allocation. The size and scope of combatant command J–8's will vary according to the command's mission and especially so for the functional commands, SOCOM [United States Special Operations Command], STRATCOM [United States Strategic Command], and TRANSCOM [United States Transportation Command].

In reviews of major headquarters, I recommend that DOD and Congress review the purpose and size of these combatant command J–8 functions to ensure they are not duplicating program and resource activities that are primarily the responsibility of others.

For reasons outlined in more detail in my testimony, I do not believe we need to establish more services. In response to new technologies or the need for new capabilities, I would observe that creating new staff organizations, agencies, and command arrangements has thus far proven to be more attractive and flexible over time.

However, I do believe the existing service headquarters could be more effective and efficient, and I support the consolidation of the secretariat and service staffs within each military department.

Current arrangements have a long history and a benefit of strong alignment with the existing structure of a separate OSD [the Office of the Secretary of Defense] with its under secretaries and joint staff with a common military staff structure. Nonetheless, the abiding presence of two staffs in the same headquarters, three in the Department of the Navy, has periodically been a source of both tension and confusion both internally within the respective services and externally to those with whom the services interact. It is duplicative in several areas and generally inefficient.

Consolidation of military department headquarters staffs has been in the 'good idea but too hard' box for many years and it will require a careful approach. It has a long history with great potential for missteps. Congress should take a deliberate approach, provide time for the services to carefully prepare legislative proposals and take a close look at the details before signing up to the concept. As much as possible, Congress should also provide for uniformity across the military department headquarters, as was done in Goldwater-Nichols, while accommodating the special circumstances of two services in the Department of the Navy.

With respect to combatant commands, I have views on the current unified command plan but no recommendations for increasing or decreasing the number or type of commands except to note that for the past 15 years it appears that DOD has been self-limiting the total number of such commands at about nine to ten.

Taking the number and type of combatant commands as roughly correct, I believe the preferred way to manage them is to maintain close control over their assigned forces and low-density/high-demand assets and how well these commands' staffs are resourced. Congress should expect DOD to carefully review the size of combatant command headquarters and each of their staff directorates and make choices on which to staff more or less robustly according to their mission and current needs.

Sizing decisions for staff directorates need to accommodate differences in combatant command missions and between the combatant commands and other components. In addition to the differences in the J–8 functions that I mentioned, the combatant command J–1 personnel office, for example, performs a substantially smaller and more discrete personnel function than you find in military departments.

Finally, any review of combatant command headquarters should ensure that all of these commands maintain sufficient resources to support their core capabilities for planning and executing joint operations.

Joint intelligence operation centers and regional centers for security studies such as the Marshall Center in EUCOM [United States European Command] and the Asia-Pacific Center in PACOM [United States Pacific Command] also deserve close attention. These are subordinate components or direct reporting units, technically not part of the combatant commands' headquarters, but nonetheless resource-intensive elements within the commands' scope of responsibilities.

I strongly support the alignment of these intelligence and security study centers within their respective commands, but due to their size, I recommend that they be revalidated as necessary and appropriate in combatant commands.

More important, Mr. Chairman, than how many or what type of commands DOD has is how well they work together, which is a matter of increasing urgency given the current security environment. Today's environment requires us to take joint commands to new levels of operational competency, including more coordination and collaboration with U.S. Government agencies and increasing collaboration with international partners and allies. We need to move in these directions if possible without increasing the total number of personnel in combatant command headquarters.

I recommend that DOD and Congress support the evolution of combatant command headquarters to accommodate these increasing requirements.

We also need to recognize that in this environment, cross-domain, cross-regional, and cross-functional operations put higher demands on our ability to integrate the work of multiple combatant commands, further complicating the web of supported and supporting command relationships. In this context, the U.S. needs to enhance strategic planning for global operations in which multiple regional and functional commands will be operating simultaneously. In the midst of this demanding environment, we need robust gaming, joint training and exercises across combatant commands that will facilitate the test and evaluation of new operating concepts and validate plans.

In the aftermath of disestablishing JFCOM [Joint Forces Command], I recommend that Congress ask DOD what it has in place as the mechanisms and resources for joint experimentation.

We must also act to ensure the necessary responsibilities, authorities, and resources are in place for the Chairman of the Joint Chiefs to effectively integrate the combatant commands' planning activities on a dynamic and global basis.

I recommend that this committee and DOD work together to ensure the responsibility for development of strategic integrated planning across all combatant commands is properly assigned with the necessary authorities and resources to support this work.

Mr. Chairman, Congress should partner with DOD in all this work and choose carefully and jointly to set priorities to generate mutual confidence and enhance prospects for successful implementation of any resulting reforms. Not all improvements require statutory changes, and many opportunities for improvement fall within DOD's existing authorities.

There will always be a need for greater efficiency in DOD, and I commend the DOD leadership and Congress for keeping up this pressure. Transferring the savings from headquarters efficiencies and other reforms to combat capabilities is a model we should pursue, but we should also keep in mind that these savings and efficiencies alone will not close the business case. To meet the demands of the current strategic environment and support the warfighters today and tomorrow, DOD will need more resources and flexibility to sustain and in some areas increase capacity to rebuild readiness and to modernize the force.

Mr. Chairman, thank you for this opportunity to present my views. Again, thank you for this important series of hearings that you have kicked off. I look forward to your questions.

[The prepared statement of Mr. Donley follows:]

PREPARED STATEMENT BY MICHAEL B. DONLEY

SUPPORTING THE WARFIGHTER OF TODAY AND TOMORROW

Thank you, Chairman McCain and Ranking Member Reed for holding this series of hearings. My testimony will focus on the roles and relationships between Military Departments and the Combatant Commands, and two areas—command arrangements and resource allocation—where these components interact to produce warfighting capabilities. I suggest specific areas for DoD and congressional review and also offer other recommendations for reducing resource intensive Military Department and Combatant Command headquarters, and better preparing joint and Service headquarters for the demanding 21st century security environment. The context for these recommendations is Section 346 of the FY16 National Defense Authorization Act, which requires DoD to report on planned reductions to its major headquarters activities by March, 2016.

MILITARY DEPARTMENTS

The role of Military Departments is to recruit, organize, train, and equip (OT&E) forces for assignment to Combatant Commands. The three Military Departments, composed of four Services, are organized around the land, maritime, and aerospace domains. [1] These are DoD's largest operating components with the longest history and they serve as the foundation for the U.S. military—the places from which the full scope of military capabilities are derived and sustained.

In the broader scheme of defense organization, the Services maintain critical relationships with OSD and the Joint Staff, DoD's two staff components whose broad purpose is to advise the Secretary of Defense on strategic direction of the armed forces. The Services must also maintain relationships with the 28 Defense Agencies and DoD Field Activities that provide centralized support. [2] In these relationships, the Services are both customers of such agencies, and also providers of uniformed personnel and other resources to those same agencies. Most importantly, the Services must maintain close relationships with the warfighters, the nine Combatant

---

[1] For simplicity, this paper will hereafter refer to Military Departments as "Services" and summarize their common functions as "OT&E" responsibilities. Descriptions of component responsibilities are from Title 10, U.S. Code, and DoD Directive 5100.01, *Functions of the Department of Defense and Its Major Components*, December 2010.

[2] This paper will hereafter refer to these collectively as "Defense Agencies".

Commands that conduct joint operations with forces assigned by the Secretary of Defense from the Services.

Service Strengths and Weaknesses. The Services are the primary and best sources of expertise on their respective domains of warfare; on the training and readiness status of their forces; on force and weapon system capabilities and limitations; and on tactics, techniques, and procedures for force and weapon system-level employment. They are essential sources of advice for Combatant Commanders charged with integrating the best mix of capabilities to fulfill their assigned missions, and all DoD components depend on the Services' deep institutional knowledge and technical expertise.

In programming and executing roughly 80% of DoD's budget, the broad scope of the Services' OT&E responsibilities and military functions provides the first level of integration in assessing the appropriate balance of capabilities and resources. This includes the size and composition of the force (i.e. multiple military functions and force elements) and the balance between today's readiness and investments for the future. Given the resources available, it is the Services that must balance capacity across military functions, among and between active duty and reserve components, between personnel and equipment, between combat and support elements, between training and readiness and quality of life, and between current operations and acquisition of new technology for the future. All must be considered, weighed, and provided for in proper balance.

Despite the central role of the Services in defense organization, DoD is so large and complex that, institutionally, the Services can be lacking in joint or defense-wide perspectives. For example, Service personnel sometimes lack a full appreciation for the role of Defense Agencies, seeming to overlook that this is where they get their Intelligence support, fuel to operate their equipment, health care, education for their children in remote locations, and their paycheck, among other things.

More importantly, the Services often lack the ability to convince each other that, as a Service, they can impartially and effectively lead other Services in joint activities, or perform defense-wide roles as executive agents for the Secretary of Defense. Goldwater-Nichols' emphasis on joint education and joint experience as preconditions for advancement to senior assignments, and over 30 years of combat experience under joint commands, have done much to strengthen joint perspectives in the Services, but not so much that effective joint operations could be assured if there were no Unified Combatant Commands.

MILITARY DEPARTMENTS AND COMBATANT COMMANDS: SUPPORTING THE WARFIGHTER
OF TODAY AND TOMORROW

The role of Combatant Commands is to provide authoritative direction and exercise command over assigned forces to carry out assigned missions. This includes authoritative direction over all aspects of military operations, joint training, and logistics; and prescribing command relationships, assigning functions to subordinate commanders, and employing assigned forces. DoD's nine Combatant Commands include six regional commands (NORTHCOM, SOUTHCOM, PACOM, EUCOM, CENTCOM, and AFRICOM) and three functional commands (TRANSCOM, STRATCOM, and SOCOM).

Combatant Commanders are in the operational chain of command, which runs from the President to the Secretary of Defense, and from the Secretary of Defense to the Combatant Commanders. The Chairman, JCS, among other roles, transmits communications to and from the President and Secretary of Defense to the Combatant Commanders, and vice versa. The CJCS also oversees the Combatant Commands and serves as their spokesman, especially on the operational requirements of their commands.

The Services interact with Combatant Commands in many ways on many levels to support joint operations. I would highlight two—command relationships and resource allocation—as representative of how Services support the warfighters of today and tomorrow.

Command Relationships are at the intersection of how Combatant Commands choose to organize subordinate commands, and how Services internally organize and present forces.

In general, regional Combatant Commands choose to organize forces in Land, Maritime, and Air domains within their assigned area; but both regional and functional Combatant Commands also task organize, with sub-unified commands or task forces for sub-regions, specific missions or functions.

Within the Air Force, Major Commands (MAJCOMs) exercise administrative command of Service forces in a regional or functional area, overseeing *inter alia* assigned units and personnel, training, logistical support, installations and housing, programming and budget execution, and administration of military justice. MAJCOMs may also be designated as component commands of the Combatant Commands, presenting a single face and administrative command structure through which to provide forces. For example, AF Special Operations Command is also the AF component command to SOCOM.

Within the MAJCOMs, Numbered Air Forces (NAFs) provide the operational level of command that are often designated or assigned joint operational responsibilities by the Combatant Commander. Within Pacific Air Forces, for example, the Commander, 5th AF is dual-hatted as the Commander, United States Forces, Japan. Within AF Space Command, the Commander, 14th AF is designated by STRATCOM as the Joint Functional Component Commander for Space.

These "dual-hatting" relationships make great sense as an efficient way to bridge the Service and Combatant Command command elements. At the same time, they deserve close scrutiny to ensure there is no unnecessary layering or duplication and, within the Services, that MAJCOM- and NAF-equivalent responsibilities are well-defined.

Secretary Gates' 2011 mandate for greater efficiencies spurred the Air Force to re-examine its headquarters overhead at all levels, including the Secretariat and Air Staff, MAJCOMs, NAFs, and down to the Wing level.

Numerous reductions and realignments were made in the Secretariat and Air Staff, and some functions were moved to Field Operating Activities or assigned to MAJCOMs, with overall net reductions in personnel.

Personnel management functions at the Wing and MAJCOM levels were moved and consolidated within the Air Force Personnel Center. MAJCOM installation support functions, along with separate services, contracting, and engineering agencies, were moved and consolidated in a new AF Installation & Mission Support Center attached to Air Force Materiel Command.

NAFs were restructured, focused in part on situations where MAJCOM and NAF headquarters were co-located. As a result, PACAF and USAFE eliminated 13th and 17th AF respectively, realigning their functions within the MAJCOM headquarters with a net reduction in personnel and general officer billets. These changes were coordinated with the respective Combatant Commanders to ensure consistency with the Commanders' organizational scheme for subordinate commands.

The Air Force also consolidated various ISR units and intelligence support activities into a new NAF – 25th AF, assigned to Air Combat Command, providing better, cleaner force presentation to all Combatant Commands and the Intelligence Community for ISR support.

All these changes resulted in net personnel reductions enabling the AF to achieve an overall 20% reduction in its major headquarters activities as one part of the 5-year, $34 billion in AF efficiencies achieved under Secretary Gates' initiative.

In summary, the intersection of Service and Combatant Command command relationships is critical to the proper alignment of Service forces under unified command. The Services need to create internal command arrangements that satisfy both efficiency in their administrative command and OT&E responsibilities, and effectiveness in their presentation of forces and in satisfying the operational command requirements as defined by the nine Combatant Commanders.

Reviewing this intersection between the command relationships of four Services and nine Combatant Commands is very pertinent to Congressional and DoD interest in improving the efficiency of DoD's major headquarters activities.

Recommendation: DoD and Congress review Service and Combatant Command command relationships, with four important caveats. 1) Avoid generalizations: command relationships are unique to each Service and Combatant Command. 2) Don't assume that complex command arrangements reflect duplicative or unnecessary staff: dual-hatting (even triple-hatting where allies are involved) often makes good sense. 3) Don't assume opportunities for major savings: review and take stock of previously harvested savings and efficiencies. 4) Congress should not legislate command relationships.

Resource Allocation: Balancing Today's Readiness and Tomorrow's Capabilities. Warfighter needs are expressed through multiple channels in the Planning, Programming, Budgeting, and Execution (PPBE) system– DoD's primary resource allocation process. For example, Combatant Commands express needs through Requests for Forces (RFFs), Integrated Priority Lists (IPLs), and Joint Urgent Operational Needs (JUONs), and occasionally in less formal submissions as well. Service component commanders and staff bring insights into the Combatant Commands' force and capability requirements from their Service and, in effect, advocate for the

Combatant Commanders' needs in developing the Service's annual Program Objectives Memorandum (POM).

At the DoD level, the Chairman, Joint Chiefs of Staff is charged with integrating the Combatant Commanders' needs, serving as their spokesman; preparing resource constrained strategic plans; advising the Secretary of Defense on strengths and deficiencies in force capabilities, force and capability requirements; and (when necessary) providing the Secretary with alternative program and budget recommendations that would better conform to Combatant Command needs. The Chairman does this through various channels, including the Joint Staff Directorate for Force Structure, Resources, and Assessment (J–8), a critical link with OSD's Director of Cost Assessment and Program Evaluation (CAPE) as OSD and the Joint Staff together review Service program and budget proposals in the PPBE process.

Among the critical resource allocation choices for the Services are those between the capacity and readiness of today's forces, and investing in more modern capabilities for the future; and Combatant Commands are customers for both.

To the extent today's needs are not being met due to shortages (e.g. Low Density / High Demand (LD/HD) forces), Combatant Commands favor building more capacity, because more capacity would increase their prospects for receiving more assigned forces, and for mission success. Combatant Commanders also expect that forces assigned from the Services are ready, not lacking in training or sustainability; and that the Services will fulfill this obligation. Especially in the current strategic environment, where there are multiple on-going operations and high demand for forces, sustaining capacity and readiness are urgent Combatant Command needs.

To the extent Combatant Commands can see and understand the benefits of future capabilities or technologies, they favor their development and acquisition. But here, the Combatant Commands are largely dependent on the connectivity between their Service components, Service R&D elements, and the Defense Advanced Research Projects Agency (DARPA) to keep them informed of emerging technologies and their potential benefit to future operational capability. Combatant Commanders and staffs also understand that the Services and DARPA may be seeking their endorsement for new programs to gain advantage in the broader competition for scarce resources. As new technologies mature, the Joint Requirements Oversight Council (JROC) and its link with the USD(AT&L) in the acquisition process, provide additional Joint input during review of Service-proposed procurement programs.

The bottom line, however, is that while Combatant Commands play an important role in setting demand signals by defining force and capability requirements, and are consumers of ready forces, strategic decisions on how to allocate resources and risks ultimately belong to the Secretary of Defense based on the advice of his OSD principal staff assistants and military advisors (i.e. the CJCS/JCS/Joint Staff), and the Services' senior civilian leadership.

Overall, DoD's ability to support the warfighters of today and tomorrow is dependent on sufficient appropriations from Congress. But in the context of roles and functions across DoD's major headquarters activities, these assigned responsibilities and the organizational relationships established in DoD's key management processes ensure there is joint input and review in Service resource allocation and acquisition. They provide Combatant Commands a necessary link and voice, but are also intended to keep Combatant Commands focused on their deterrence, warfighting, planning, and engagement responsibilities, minimizing the need for these headquarters to have large programming staffs duplicating the work of their Service force providers.

At the same time, the Combatant Commands need J–8 functions to interact with the Joint Staff and Services on matters related to program evaluation and resource allocation. The size and scope of Combatant Command J–8s will vary according to the command's mission, and especially so for the functional commands—SOCOM, STRATCOM, and TRANSCOM.

> *Recommendation: In review of major headquarters activities, recommend DoD and Congress review the purpose and size of Combatant Command J–8 functions to ensure they are not duplicating program and resource activities that are the primary responsibilities of others.*

OTHER ISSUES CONCERNING MILITARY DEPARTMENTS AND COMBATANT COMMANDS

Do We Need to Establish New Services for Space, Cyber, or Special Operations? Periodically, it is asked whether we need to create new Services in response to a rapidly changing technology and security environment. There is no agreed test or threshold for establishing a new Service, nor is there a clear and consistent history that suggests when this organizational option is appropriate. In 1947, for example, the Department of the Air Force was established in response to 40 years of rapid, astonishing advances in aviation technology and the progressive growth and evolution of air doctrine, culture, and organization within the U.S. Army. But there was no new Service created with the discovery of nuclear fission, or when further advances in aviation and missile technology opened up the domain of space.

Institutional responses to new threats or technology can take many forms. Important factors to consider might include:

- Maturity of the mission / function / domain and readiness to assume the full scope of OT&E functions performed by the Services (e.g. doctrine, training, logistics, infrastructure, R&D, Procurement, etc.)

- Relative size in personnel needs / resources—Does this exceed the capabilities, or is it overwhelming other military functions, of the existing Service host(s)? And,

- Whether this activity can be separated out of the Services without disrupting their ability to fulfill other assigned functions.

Often, the motivation for a new component is more attention and more money: the belief that a new component out from under its current host, reporting directly to the Secretary of Defense, would be more likely to get the management attention and resources perceived by its advocates as essential to a new, important area.

The arguments in favor of a new Service would be that it requires dedicated, component-level focus, resources, and leadership for critical capabilities that would otherwise receive insufficient attention within a larger component with multiple responsibilities. As a central feature of DoD's organizational design, however, establishment of a new Service has been and should remain a very high threshold, and we should consider all the alternatives.

If the needs related to this activity were oriented toward the integration of its warfighting elements, then new command arrangements in the joint system might be a better solution. Alternatively, where new, emerging needs are focused on supporting capabilities and more efficient resource management with more business and less military content, then a Defense Agency might be an appropriate course of action. Importantly, whatever structural or organizational solution(s) are considered best, linkages with the roles and responsibilities of other DoD staffs and components should be identified, de-conflicted, and made clear.

Given the current management and resource environment, however, I find the arguments opposing new Services more persuasive. Further sub-division of the four Services to create another Service would yield more headquarters, duplicating OT&E and staff functions already provided for; and each new component further complicates the coordination required among and across DoD's approximately 45 components. Any new Service would further spread scarce budget resources across more organizations and weaken integrated decision-making. This would further complicate the work of DoD leadership, pushing more resource tradeoffs upwards to the Secretary and Deputy Secretary of Defense.

In each of the cases at issue (space, cyber, and special operations), DoD has made reasonable choices focused on the integration of warfighting capabilities, creating joint command arrangements and leaving the development of capabilities and OT&E responsibilities to the four Services.

Creation of a new Service seems a deeper, more expensive, and more permanent commitment. In recent practice, in response to new technologies or the need for new capabilities, creating new staff functions, agencies, and command arrangements has thus far proven to be more attractive and flexible over time.

Can the Services be operated more effectively and/or efficiently? I support consolidation of the Secretariat and Service staffs within each Military Department to promote greater effectiveness and efficiency.

Current arrangements have a long history and the benefit of strong alignment with the existing structure of a separate OSD and Joint Staff at the DoD level, with their undersecretaries and a common military staff structure, respectively. Nonetheless, the abiding presence of two staffs in the same headquarters (three in the Department of the Navy) has periodically been a source of both tension and confusion, both internally within the respective Services, and externally to those with whom the Services interact. It is duplicative in several areas and, generally, inefficient.

Various recommendations for reduction or elimination of staff duplication in the Service headquarters were proposed by the 1960 Symington Committee, the 1970 Blue Ribbon Defense Panel, and the 1978 Ignatius Report. During the consideration of Goldwater-Nichols, House legislative drafts favored the integration of Service headquarters while the Senate opposed it; and the final agreement left separate staffs intact with some changes. The 1995 Commission on Roles and Missions of the Armed Forces concluded that Service Secretaries and Chiefs would be better served by a single staff of experienced civilians and uniformed officers; and the *2004 CSIS Beyond Goldwater-Nichols* Phase 1 Report echoed this recommendation.

Some useful changes have been made without legislation. Indeed, current law provides some flexibility for Service Secretaries to assign and/or move functions between the two staffs. Since 2002, the Army has sought a closer integration of its two headquarters staffs through General Orders. A recent Air Force decision to move it's A–8 programming function to the Assistant Secretary for Financial Management was a sensible step that closed a seam between programming and budgeting databases—providing more coherence and efficiency in resource allocation and budget execution. However, more fundamental changes offering greater effectiveness and efficiency will require changes in law.

Consolidation of the Service headquarters staffs within individual Military Departments would help eliminate some unnecessary or counter-productive seams. For example, separation of the Secretariats' Acquisition functions from Service staffs' Logistics functions runs counter to sound life-cycle management for weapon systems. In this instance, staff consolidations could potentially present a single Service office to interact with the USD(AT&L), and with the Services' own major commands which perform both acquisition and logistics functions. Another example is the unnecessary effort to distinguish policy and oversight in the Secretariats from Service staffs' management of nearly identical functional areas of responsibility, such as Assistant Secretaries for Manpower and Reserve Affairs, and Deputy Chiefs of Staff for Personnel.

Historically, when the subject of consolidation has arisen in the past, the civilian appointees are concerned the military staff is trying to eliminate the Secretariat, and the uniformed military is concerned the presence of civilian appointees in a single staff will interfere with what they perceive as a clear command chain within the military Service staff. The results have been strained civil-military relations and only limited progress toward greater efficiency.

Going forward, once again considering consolidation, Congress could increase the prospects for success by sustaining the principles of effective civilian control and independent military advice and ensuring Service Secretaries and Chiefs of Staff have universal access to all elements of the single headquarters staff.

The system of civilian Service secretaries and assistant secretaries should be retained because they are net value added to the Secretary of Defense and to the Service headquarters. While it is true that the Secretary of Defense exercises civilian control through delegated authority to Under Secretaries of Defense and other OSD officials in various functional areas, none of these Under Secretaries has the full scope of responsibilities necessary to oversee a Military Department. Working together in the most optimistic circumstances, these OSD officials bring many disparate views to the table. In short, I do not believe the Secretary of Defense can exercise effective civilian control over Military Departments through the OSD staff alone.

Based on my experience in both OSD and the Air Force, the size and scope of the Military Departments and the issues that arise within them warrant a parallel structure of civilian control in OSD and the Services. Ensuring the Secretary of Defense's direction and intent is understood and implemented at the Service level, overseeing the promotion and assignment of senior personnel, overseeing resource allocation and program execution, and holding senior civilian and military officials accountable for their performance and conduct are among the leadership functions that benefit from strong civilian control within the Military Department headquarters.

Provide the Service Chief unfettered access to any and all Military Department headquarters staff for the purpose of developing military advice as a member of the Joint Chiefs of Staff. This is an essential element of any Service headquarters consolidation and can be accomplished through a legislative provision to that effect. Specifically, it would ensure that the Service chief would have access to military personnel within any staff function without interference, regardless of whether such function is led by an Assistant Secretary or another senior civilian. In practice, this should present no issue since the Plans and Operations functions on the military staff have no counterpart in the Service Secretariats and would likely continue to be led by General/Flag Officers.

Maintain a Mix of Appointees, Uniformed Personnel, and Career Civilians. In addition, it is important to recognize that creating a single headquarters staff is not a choice between civilian or military staffs. The Secretariats include many uniformed officers, including senior officers in functions designated in law as the sole responsibility of the Secretary—for example, Acquisition, Financial Management, Legislative Affairs, and Public Affairs. Likewise, the military staff contains Senior

Executive Service civilians who provide deep expertise and continuity, compensating for the high personnel turnover associated with military rotations. Civilian appointees bring different and useful DoD, congressional, or industry experience and skill sets, currently atypical in a military career, that complement those of uniformed leaders and career civilians.

In my experience, the Service Secretary benefits from a strong partnership with the Service Chief, and the Service Chief benefits from having a strong civilian partner in the Service Secretary. Overall, the Service headquarters benefits from this mix of political appointees, uniformed personnel, and career civilians.

Consolidation of Military Department headquarters staffs has been in the "good idea, but too hard" box for many years and will require a careful approach. It has a long history and great potential for missteps. Congress should take a deliberate approach, provide time for the Services to carefully prepare legislative proposals, and take a closer look at the details before signing up to the concept. Congress should, as much as possible, also provide for uniformity across the Military Department headquarters as was done during Goldwater-Nichols, while accommodating the special circumstances of two Services in the Department of the Navy.

> ***Recommendation: Consolidate Military Department headquarters staffs as proposed to help improve unity of effort, effectiveness, and efficiency; and present a single Service headquarters structure to the field. Retain the benefits of strong civilian alignment with OSD and military alignment with the Joint Staff and other military staffs.***

Does DoD Need More, or Fewer, Combatant Commands? The U.S. military needs Unified Combatant Commands. Over 60 years of combat experience has proven that no single service can conduct effective operations without assistance from others, and more recent experience demonstrates that 21st century warfare crosses multiple domains and regions.

Moreover, we have tried the alternatives. Experience showed that "specified" combatant commands led by a single service (e.g. Strategic Air Command and Military Airlift Command) did not produce sufficient integration of effort and, of necessity, needed to evolve to a higher, unified level. Ad hoc task forces for multi-service operations did not work as well as joint commands with trained staffs and a full-time focus on joint force integration (e.g. the evolution from Rapid Deployment Force to Rapid Deployment Joint Task Force to CENTCOM).

Current concerns are focused on the number of Combatant Commands and the size of their headquarters staffs.

Service Chiefs, as members of the JCS, have important roles to play in weighing the pros and cons of new joint commands and advising the Secretary of Defense. This is because any new Combatant Command will need to be staffed by personnel from across the Services. In addition, the Services act as Executive Agents for Combatant Command headquarters with responsibility for funding and administration of these activities on Service installations.[3] In this sense, the Services act as an internal brake on unconstrained growth in the joint system.

Informally, it appears DoD has been limiting its Unified Command Plan (UCP) to around 9–10 commands. The post 9/11 creation of NORTHCOM in 2002 was part of a restructuring that disestablished SPACECOM and assigned space functions to STRATCOM, resulting in no net increase in the number of commands. Importantly, other 2002 UCP changes included the assignment of countries previously outside the purview of any regional command; thus for the first time providing the UCP with global coverage.

In considering whether to split-off Africa from EUCOM's area of responsibility and find the resources for a new headquarters, the creation of AFRICOM in 2008 was 'on the cusp'. With continuing instability in the horn of Africa, the emergence of Al Qaida-affiliated groups in the Maghreb, a growing war on terrorism, and the need to develop indigenous African military capabilities, it was clear there were multiple political-military issues to address in a new command. But it was also clear that a new AFRICOM would not have assigned forces (though USSOCOM assets would routinely operate within the region), and its headquarters would be different from other commands, staffed with more non-military, interagency personnel.

In 2010, when Secretary Gates' efficiency initiatives included a review of joint headquarters, it was determined that the UCP could live without Joint Forces Command. Thus, AFRICOM was last "in" and JFCOM was last "out".

In assessing the future of the six regional commands, I would not recommend any changes. It has taken a long time to achieve global coverage in a reasonable configu-

---

[3] DoD Directive 5100.3, *Support of the Headquarters of Combatant and Subordinate Unified Commands,* February 2011.

ration, which should be considered important progress; and adjustments on the boundaries can be expected in the normal course of business. The option of merging NORTHCOM and SOUTHCOM into an ''Americas'' or ''Western Hemisphere'' command mixes very different missions and would dilute necessary focus on the homeland. Given the dynamic strategic environment in Europe, it doesn't make sense to reverse course and reassign AFRICOM to EUCOM, and the United States would pay some political price with new African partners if it did so.

Among the functional commands, CYBERCOM—currently a sub-unified command within STRATCOM—appears poised to emerge as the tenth Combatant Command. This long-debated development involves highly complex relationships between DoD and the Intelligence Community, and within the UCP itself. Some of the UCP implications are discussed below.

What changes to the Joint system should be considered? Given this perspective that the number and type of Combatant Commands is roughly correct, the preferred way to manage them is to maintain close control over assigned forces and LD/HD assets, and how well their staffs are resourced. Congress should expect DoD to carefully review the size of Combatant Command headquarters and each of their staff directorates, and make choices on which to staff more or less robustly according to their mission and need.

I would not recommend DoD change, nor Congress legislate, staff structure (i.e. J–1 thru J-x). The existing structure provides an important, common framework across all military staffs and provides basis for communication and process interaction in both operational and administrative contexts. Sizing decisions for staff directorates simply need to accommodate differences in Combatant Command missions, and between the Combatant Commands and other components. In addition to differences in the J–8 functions previously discussed, for example, a Combatant Command J–1 (personnel office) performs a substantially smaller and more discrete personnel function than is found in Military Departments. Finally, any such review of Combatant Command headquarters should ensure all commands maintain sufficient resources to support their core capabilities for planning and executing joint operations.

Joint Intelligence Operations Centers and the regional centers for security studies, such as the George C. Marshall Center in EUCOM, and the Asia-Pacific Center in PACOM, also deserve close attention. These are subordinate components or direct-reporting units, technically not part of the Combatant Commands' headquarters but nonetheless resource-intensive elements within Combatant Commands' scope of responsibilities. I strongly support the alignment of these intelligence and security studies centers within their respective commands. Nonetheless, due to their size, I recommend they be re-validated as necessary and appropriate for Combatant Commands.

> ***Recommendation: DoD and Congress should review the size and composition of each Combatant Command headquarters and their supporting elements.***

Just as President Eisenhower noted in 1958, and Goldwater-Nichols later reinforced, that *''Separate ground, sea, and air warfare is gone forever ... ''* we should recognize today that single theater warfare has been rapidly fading in the shadow of trans-national threats and globalization. In addition, new and more demanding roles for Combatant Commands have emerged that should be recognized and accommodated.

More important than how many or what type of commands DoD has is how well they work together—a matter of increasing urgency given the current security environment.

Hybrid warfare, constant cyber attacks, and terrorists and non-state actors with global reach crisscross artificial regional command boundaries and keep CYBERCOM and SOCOM continuously engaged in world-wide operations. Attacks on the United States could well begin in the silent domains of space and cyber with effects in NORTHCOM's area of responsibility. Regional military commands are but one element in a larger fabric of United States Government and international engagement and collaboration in meeting contemporary challenges and threats to international security.

The Combatant Commands' role in ''engagement'' has evolved since the 1986 enactment of Goldwater-Nichols. They are still responsible for integrating joint U.S. combat and support capabilities, but now in addition they are serving as senior U.S. military representatives in developing international partners and conducting planning for coalition operations. This role helps extend the international reach of the CJCS in counterpart relations, providing for more regular interaction with regional allies and partners at the strategic level, and deeper military-to-military relationships in critical areas such as missile defense.

I strongly endorse this role for the Combatant Commanders. Critics note the U.S. military can become too dominant in regional affairs that more properly belong to the State Department. Where that may occur, the answer is not to diminish the military engagement, but to increase diplomatic and other interagency capabilities and resources necessary to support the full scope of U.S. interests in the region.

Today's security environment requires us to take joint commands to new levels of operational competency, including more coordination and collaboration with other U.S. Government agencies, and increasing collaboration with international partners and allies. We need to move in these directions, if possible, without increasing the total number of personnel in Combatant Command headquarters.

> *Recommendation: DoD and Congress should support the evolution of Combatant Command headquarters to accommodate increasing collaboration with U.S. Government agencies and international partners.*

We also need to recognize that, in the current security environment, cross-domain, cross-regional, and cross-functional operations put higher demands on our ability to integrate the work of multiple Combatant Commands, further complicating the web of "supported-supporting" command relationships.

Within the current UCP, STRATCOM, in addition to its foundational mission of nuclear deterrence, has multiple global missions/responsibilities to bring to bear, including Space, Global C4ISR, Cyber, Counter-WMD, Global Missile Defense, and Global Strike. Much-needed, integrated perspectives on how these domains and missions should be defended and exploited in today's complex environment are still in development. Under current arrangements, while the relationships among STRATCOM's many global missions and their "supporting-supported" relationships to other Combatant Commands have not been developed to their full potential, these global tools have at least been kept in the same Command bag. Thus, any realignment of global functions (such as CYBER) away from STRATCOM will create additional command seams that will need to be addressed.

In this context, the U.S. needs to enhance strategic planning for global operations in which multiple regional and functional commands will be operating simultaneously. In the midst of this demanding environment, we need robust gaming, joint training, and exercises across Combatant Commands that will facilitate the test and evaluation of new operating concepts and validate plans.

> *Recommendation: In the aftermath of disestablishing JFCOM, Congress should ask whether DoD has in place the mechanisms and resources for joint experimentation.*

The question arises: who has the responsibility for integrating the Combatant Commands' work and do they have sufficient authority and resources for this purpose? In my judgment, the Chairman, JCS, in coordination with the USD(P), has the responsibility and sufficient authority for this work. The Chairman is responsible for overseeing the Combatant Commands, for being their spokesman, and for developing resource constrained strategic plans. The Chairman establishes rules and procedures for the Joint community, including areas such as the Joint Strategic Planning System, and Joint Doctrine. The Chairman also functions within the chain of command and assists the President and Secretary of Defense in their command functions.

Together, I believe these assigned duties are sufficient for the Chairman to coordinate and direct the integration of Combatant Command planning; and if not, sufficient authority is only a short distance away through a targeted delegation of authority from the Secretary of Defense. A contrary view, however, is that the Chairman needs to be in the chain of command—requiring a change in law—to exercise this authority.

> *Recommendation: DoD and Congress ensure the responsibility for development of strategic, integrated planning across all Combatant Commands is properly assigned with the necessary authorities and resources to support this work.*

CONCLUSION

I support the consolidation of Service headquarters staffs, and reviews of Service and Combatant Command command arrangements, and Combatant Command staffs and support components, for greater efficiencies. [4] We must also act to ensure the necessary responsibilities, authorities, and resources are in place within the joint system to meet the demands of the current security environment.

Congress should partner with DoD in all this work, choose carefully and jointly to set priorities, generate mutual confidence, and enhance prospects for successful implementation of any resulting reforms. Not all improvements require new law, and many opportunities for improvement fall within DoD's existing authorities.

However, the biggest problems in supporting the warfighter are not in the headquarters, they are in the corridors of Congress. Specifically, the inability of Congress to reach consensus on stable funding for defense sufficient to respond to a rapidly changing threat environment, improve readiness, and finance badly needed modernization across the force; and Congressional opposition to base closures and force structure adjustments recommended by military leaders that would permit the Services to shift scarce resources to meet changing needs and accelerate the acquisition of new capabilities.

There will always be a need for greater efficiency in DoD, and I commend the DoD leadership and Congress for keeping up this pressure. There will always be shortages: we have never had the resources needed to do everything that prudent and cautious military leaders think necessary to do. Transferring the savings from headquarters efficiencies and other reforms to combat capabilities is a model we should pursue, but these savings and efficiencies alone will not close the business case. To meet the demands of the current strategic environment and support the warfighters of today and tomorrow, DoD will need more resources and flexibility to sustain and in some areas increase capacity, to rebuild readiness, and to modernize the force.

Thank you for this opportunity to present my views.

Chairman McCAIN. General Flynn?

STATEMENT OF LIEUTENANT GENERAL MICHAEL T. FLYNN, USA, RETIRED, FORMER DIRECTOR OF THE DEFENSE INTELLIGENCE AGENCY

Mr. FLYNN. Thank you, Mr. Chairman. Chairman McCain, Ranking Member Reed, thanks. Great seeing you again.

I actually was a lieutenant and my first combat experience was in Grenada in 1983. So it is interesting that I am sitting here today because it was a mess. It was very confusing.

Thanks for inviting me to participate alongside these other great patriots.

Chairman McCAIN. Good thing it was not a formidable opponent, do you not think?

Mr. FLYNN. Yes. I have a few choice words today for the Cubans.

Anyway, I appreciate sitting aside these two really unbelievable patriots of our country and longtime servants and to really just offer some thoughts on this defense reform. I hope that I offer thoughts that I think that are going to be consistent with the other themes that you have already heard from other people that have testified, as well as I think today maybe I will add a few new ideas.

In the times that we face and we will likely face in this very complex and unpredictable world, addressing defense reform is probably the single biggest strategic issue that we must deal with, and I believe we have to deal with it immediately.

The days of large organizations moving at the speed of an elephant with bulky, expensive, overly bureaucratic acquisition programs with little value to our warfighters and even less value to our national security are forever gone.

Speed is the new big. Innovation is the new norm. The pace of change is so stunningly fast, and the Defense Department, at least

---

[4] While not considered for this hearing, I also recommend close review of OSD, Joint Staff, and Defense Agency headquarters.

inside the Pentagon, is not capable of meeting the demands of future threats.

Rearranging the deck chairs on this Titanic will only make the chairs slide in a different direction on that deck, but the ship will still likely sink.

As you said, Chairman, former Secretary Robert Gates stated it best. I think it was in the fall of 2008 is when he said it, that the Pentagon is good at planning for war, but on its best day cannot fight a war. That has been proven in spades over the past decade and a half with few exceptions.

If the past 14 years of conflict have proven anything, it has proven Secretary Gates to be spot-on when it came to making that fateful statement.

Neither our Nation nor the citizens our defense system is designed to protect and defend can operate in the future the way we operate today.

I would add that even though a nice glossy and well meaning report will come out of this committee, there are people inside the Department—and I am serious about this—that are looking at your efforts today as a joke and wondering why do you bother, nothing will ever change. Please, Chairman and members of this committee, please prove them wrong.

We have forgotten how to win wars because we have lost sight of what winning looks like. Instead, we plod along, participating in conflict and allowing an overly bulky and bureaucratic Department of Defense and a completely broken interagency process, led by the White House and rightly so, that has choked itself practically to death. It simply does not work in support of our warfighting needs today. The President in his role as commander-in-chief and the Secretary of Defense in his role as leader of our defense establishment are ill-served. There is no soft or kind way of saying that. In a giant organization like the Department of Defense, change is not easy. Reforms will take time, and I applaud this committee's efforts to give it your best shot.

At the end of the day, still the budget process and not the mission is what truly changes anything in our government. We have to reverse that thinking particularly when it comes to defense. That is just simply the sad truth. Where the money goes, things happen. Despite where that money goes, most times has no bearing on our ability to win wars. If you do not get any money, you either change or you disappear. If you get money, you are able to survive another day.

My experience comes serving over 33 years in uniform, 12 in joint assignments, and nearly 10 of those as a flag officer. I have also served many years in combat and have suffered from the lack of many capabilities that we needed to fight our enemies and found myself fighting the Pentagon as much or more than our enemies. The bureaucracy of our lethargic system filled with people who depart for the day from their major headquarters or from the Pentagon and leave an inbox filled with actions to await tomorrow while we were sitting in a combat zone waiting for an answer is not a good way to fight a war.

I have many personal examples and personal scars and I have witnessed many examples of this in may days deployed to the wars primarily in the Middle East and Central Asia. We must and can do better for our Nation and for those that serve this Nation.

Today I will highlight a couple of points and provide some ideas, and hopefully a few of these are new.

First, we will never correctly predict the next war. We can warn about the many threats that we face, and there are numerous and very dangerous threats. You mentioned a few in your remarks, Chairman. ISIS [the Islamic State of Iraq and Syria] is the latest in a long line of threats to our Nation that we must do more to contain, defeat, and ultimately eliminate this radical Islamist ideology. There are many more threats than this very dangerous enemy.

Second, the connection between people, processes, and systems is completely broken.

Regarding people, we recruit still using old, outdated mechanisms and tools, and then we train people with equipment that is aging, not the most advanced even though we, our country, has the most advanced technologies available to anyone in the world. Bottom line in this regard is our recruiting and training are being done with less than stellar rules, tools, and advanced capabilities. We can do better.

We force our warriors to fight wars by forcing them to push joint urgent operational needs or urgent needs statements from the battlefield up the chain of command. That is no way to fight a war. It is reality because our people do not have, they do not train with, they do not go to war with the right tools. I have seen this numerous times. Essentially they are not prepared to go to war with the equipment in our current inventories. We have to do better, and as the best military in the world, we cannot afford to not look serious to the men and women that we are supposed to serve. We do not look very professional in the eyes of our international partners, never mind our enemies.

Lastly, we must consider retooling our high-tech training. We must radically move from the information age to the digital age, and we have to do this quickly. China, for example, has an organization of 800,000 cyber warriors, and I highlight this in my statement for the record. 800,000 cyber warriors. I was just briefed on this about 2 weeks ago at a cyber training event that happened out at Camp Dawson, West Virginia. A fantastic capability. These 800,000 cyber warriors in China are associated with their Department 61398 that we all became familiar with when the Mandiant report came out. We are struggling in the Department to recruit I think 6,000 within our own Department of Defense that Mike Rogers, our great cyber commander, has highlighted as a need. That number fluctuates. But this is the problem that we are facing. Again, I will give you a little bit more information on that number. Something is wrong with that picture. Any reform must consider retooling for future jobs and not hold desperately to these 20th century tools and models that we have.

On processes, the processes that we use are antiquated and usually one war behind, if not more. I went to war in Afghanistan the first time based still on airland battle doctrine, a doctrine designed for the Cold War, originally written in the early 1980s. That doctrine was still being trained right up until 2006, 5 years into the war when Generals Petraeus and Mattis came out with the counterinsurgency manual or counterinsurgency doctrine. We can and must do better. We have to either understand the type of war that we are in and make the decisions upfront to get to where we need to be.

But why did it take us nearly 5 years to change our doctrine when we were directly engaged in a counterinsurgency and counterterrorism campaign? Two reasons are—and there are others. Bureaucracy and service parochial infighting are two of those. Thank God our superb men, women, soldiers, sailors, airmen, and marines and those civilians serving in combat innovate better than any other military in the world. When they realize that something is broken, they fix it on the battlefield instead of using the Pentagon's motto of "if it is broke, let somebody else fix it." We still need the money.

Lastly, the systems we have and the acquisition system that drives much of how our services and combatant commanders operate may as well be in separate solar systems, and none of these, with few exceptions, seem to be anywhere near the battlefields we operate on today.

It is tempting to sit here and beat up those in the Pentagon, and that would be unfair. But there are there some in our system that see a jobs program, some who have never seen a program of record they did not like, and some who abuse the system so badly that it makes corrupt governments in the Third World nations blush.

Additionally, after nearly 14 years of war, conflict, call it what you will, we are engaged with enemies of our country and they want to win. I am not certain we have demonstrated the resilience or the fortitude to do the same, at least not yet.

There are many in the defense system that have yet to experience that and do not understand the demands of combat, and there others who avoid it wishing it will go away. It will not. We, you, Chairman, committee have to fix a number of things, but one of the most important is the acquisition system, I think has been highlighted by many who have testified to this committee. It must be joint and it must include the warfighter requirements and not simply serve the service chiefs, secretaries, and their constituents' needs. Secretary Gates found this, as you highlighted, and fixed it, but to do so, he had to become the best action officer in the Pentagon.

That said, let me list a couple of ideas to consider as we go through the rest of this session and as you contemplate what steps you need to take forward. I will be prepared to address any of these in Q and A.

Number one, tooth-to-tail ration must change. Reverse it before we find ourselves not ready to fight, never mind win. We have way too much overhead and our staffs have become bloated beyond the nonsense stage.

Number two, related to the above, we have way too many four-stars, commands and otherwise, around the world and too many four-star headquarters in each of the services. In terms of our warfighting that the Secretary mentioned, we have 11 warfighting commands if you count USFK [United States Forces Korea] as a subcomponent and you count Cyber Command as a unified component. 11, not to mention the service four- and three- star positions that could easily be reduced a rank or cut and the staffs could subsequently be reduced.

Number three, cut the civilian system in half or more because the growth has just been unbelievable. I saw that in my own agency looking at 10 years of history before I even took over the Defense Intelligence Agency. Turn those dollars into readiness and place more tooth into our warfighting forces. Be cautious about salami slicing and help the SecDef [the Secretary of Defense] and the senior civilian and military leaders make the best decisions based on a unified and strategic national security vision approved by the President instead of slicing to benefit some constituency. You must play a role, but very candidly and over many years, Congress created much of this mess and now you have an opportunity and I believe a responsibility to correct it. So thank you for taking this on.

Number four, we need to seriously look at how we organize to fight and win in wars. We man, train, and equip as services, i.e., Title 10. We go to war as a joint force, and in general Air Force takes the Army, the Marines take the Navy—and again, I am generalizing there. But we only win as a coalition. We need to determine—in fact, in here I say please name one time when we did not fight as a coalition. I mean that, and if you go back in our history, even to the days of George Washington.

So we need to determine if we are creating a force that is not only technically qualified but also culturally and societally understanding and smart. Language training, for example, is something that we need to place greater emphasis on for those officers serving in maneuver and operational assignments. You know, foreign languages are not just for the intelligence community and attaches. For example, maybe we make it a prerequisite for combatant commanders to speak a foreign language before they can even be considered for a combatant command assignment. Maybe we do that for a majority of our three- and four-star assignments. That example, that message would go a long way and reverberate across the entire force, and it would change the culture all the way down to our ROTC [Reserve Officer Training Corps] programs, our junior ROTC programs, and in our service academies. It would take a generation, but I think we need to think like that.

Number five, we need to significantly increase the tenure and stature of the Chairman of the Joint Chiefs of Staff and the Vice Chairman. Tenures with a minimum of 5 years—my recommendation—without reconfirmation. It does not mean that the President cannot lose confidence and you cannot get rid of that person if they are not doing their job, but I think a tenure with a minimum of 5 years should be considered. Why 5 years? In order to last longer than the service chiefs and potentially serve or overlap two Presidents. This maintains the unbiased responsibility that the Chairman and the Vice with serving in that role as required has as the principal military advisor to the President.

Number six, conduct a thorough and comprehensive overhaul of the defense acquisition system. Look at every single program of record. Every program not currently meeting its timelines or budgets should be immediately cut. Now, that is a big statement, but when you send a message that waste and substandard performance will no longer be tolerated, that would send shockwaves through the system and my belief is it would be nearly impossible to do. It would be the harder right thing to do. I do not believe necessarily that you could do it, but it would be interesting to see how many programs in an analysis of that that are actually up to standard. There are very few exceptions or very few in my experience and in my judgment today sitting here.

Number seven, increase the investment in small businesses. Today I believe the Defense Department policy states a goal of 25 percent investments in small businesses across the Department. Small businesses are the engine of change in our country right now, and with the rapid advancement in technologies across the board from health care to intelligence, we must seek new, innovative, and disruptive ways to force fundamental change. Most on this committee would be challenged to recognize the Fortune 100, never mind Fortune 500. They are all relatively new and many started as small businesses within the last decade. As stated, small businesses also innovate. They have to in order to survive. My strongest suggestion for consideration at this stage is to increase the small business investment goals of the Department to as high as 50 percent. I believe the Department and especially our warfighters would benefit most and many would benefit overnight. Lastly, small businesses are the best way to increase our Nation's economic strength, a drive change in this country. They would help us retool our Nation for the digital age.

Number eight and the last recommendation is decide who and where decisions about acquisition reform can be made. The SecDef cannot make them all. But if a service chief comes in and says we need this program, cannot live without it, and a combatant commander comes in and says that program is not working, then do not let the system decide to keep it and only fix it on the margins. Get rid of it, or make the necessary decisions that actually make a difference. If they see something elsewhere and that is a capability they want, especially our warfighting commanders, and it can be produced in the requisite amounts within existing budgets, get it to them rapidly or allow them to acquire it without going through the whole morass of bureaucracy.

In this context, the questions that this committee is considering are in my judgment the correct ones, namely, whether our Nation's institutions of national defense are organized, manned, equipped, and managed in ways that can deal with the security challenges of the 21st century and that efficiently and effectively spend our Nation's dollars.

The Department is not meeting those challenges today, and we are not ready to deal with the challenges we, as the global leader with the premier military capability on the planet, should be capable of in the future.

Without fundamental and massive reform, as well as some smart, numerous, and targeted reductions in areas that have grown bloated, irrelevant, and useless, we could find ourselves on the losing end of a major war, Chairman, one that sitting here today we are unable to predict.

If our Nation is proud of being the world's leader, let us start acting like it and as our very first President, George Washington, stated, ''To be prepared for war is one of the most effective means of preserving peace.''

Thank you for this opportunity. I look forward to your questions. Thank you.

[The prepared statement of Mr. Flynn follows:]

THE PREPARED STATEMENT BY LTG MICHAEL T. FLYNN (RETIRED)

Chairman McCain, Senator Reed: Thank you for inviting me to participate alongside other great patriots of our country to offer some thoughts about defense reform and hope I offer thoughts consistent with many other themes you have heard from previous testimony as well as a few new ideas.

In the times we face and will likely face in this very complex and unpredictable world, addressing defense reform is probably the single biggest strategic issue we must deal with (and deal with immediately).

The days of large organizations moving at the speed of an elephant with bulky, expensive, overly bureaucratic acquisition programs, with little value to our warfighters and even less value to our national security are forever gone.

Speed is the new big. Innovation is the norm, the pace of change is so stunningly fast, and the Defense Department (at least inside the Pentagon) is not capable of meeting the Demands of the future threats.

Rearranging the deck chairs on the *Titanic* will only make the chairs slide in a different direction on the deck, but the ship will still sink.

Former Secretary Robert Gates stated it best when he said that the Pentagon is good at planning for war, but on its best day cannot fight a war (that has been proven in spades over the past decade and a half (with few exceptions).

And if the past fourteen years of conflict have proven anything, it has proven Secretary Gates to be spot on when it came to making that fateful statement.

Neither our nation nor the citizens our defense system is designed to protect and defend can operate in the future the way we operate today.

I would add that even though a nice glossy and well-meaning report will come out of this committee, there are people inside the Department that are looking at your efforts today as a joke and wondering, why do you bother ... nothing will ever change.

Please prove them wrong. We have forgotten how to win wars.

Because we have lost sight of what winning looks like, instead we plod along, participating in conflict and allowing an overly bulky and bureaucratic Department of Defense and a completely broken interagency process, led by the White House (and rightly so) that has choked itself practically to death—it simply doesn't work in support of our warfighting needs today—the president, in his role as commander-in-chief and the SecDef in his role as leader of our defense establishment are ill-served—there is no soft or kind way of saying that.

And in a giant organization like the Department of Defense, change is not easy, reforms will take time, and I applaud your efforts to give it your best shot.

At the end of the day, the budget process (and not the mission) is what truly changes anything in our government. We have to reverse that thinking.

That is the sad truth.

Where the money goes, things happen.

And despite where that money goes, most times, has no bearing on our ability to win wars.

If you don't get any money, you either change or you disappear. If you get money, you are able to survive another day.

My experience comes from serving over thirty three years in uniform, twelve in joint assignments and nearly ten of those as a flag officer.

I have also served many years in combat and have suffered from the lack of many capabilities we needed to fight our enemies and found myself fighting the Pentagon as much or more than our enemies. The bureaucracy of our lethargic system filled with people who depart for the day from their major headquarters or from the Pentagon and leave an inbox filled with actions to await tomorrow while I was sitting in a combat zone waiting for an answer ... not a good way to fight a war.

I have many personal examples and scars and have witnessed many examples of this in my days deployed to the wars in the Middle East and Central Asia.

We must and can do better.

Today, I will highlight a couple of points and provide some ideas—hopefully, a few are new:

First, we will never correctly predict the next war. We can warn about the many threats we face (and there are numerous and very dangerous threats—ISIS is the latest in a long line of threats to our nation that we must do more to contain, defeat and ultimately eliminate this radical Islamist ideology). And there are many more threats than this very dangerous enemy.

And second, the connection between people, processes and systems is completely broken.

Regarding people; we recruit using old outdated mechanisms and tools and then train people with equipment that is aging, not the most advanced, even though we (our country) have the most advanced technologies available to anyone in the world. Bottom line, our recruiting and training are being done with less than stellar rules, tools and advanced capabilities.

We force our warriors to fight wars by forcing them to push joint urgent operational needs or emergency needs statements from the battlefield up the chain—that is no way to fight a war. It is reality because our people don't have, don't train, don't go to war with, the right tools. Essentially, they are not prepared to go to war with the equipment in our current inventories.

We have to do better, and as the best military in the world, we can't afford to not look serious to the men and women we are supposed to serve and we don't look very professional in the eyes of our international partners (never mind our enemies).

Lastly, we must consider retooling our high tech training. We must radically move from the information age to the digital age. China has an organization of 800k cyber warriors* associated with their Department 61398 and we are struggling to recruit 6k in the Department (*China has approximately 800k in their Honker Army/Honker Union—this is a group—some overt, some not, affiliated with the Chinese government—*http:bbs.cnhonker.com/forum.php*—take extreme precautions going to this website). Something is wrong with that picture.

Any reform must consider retooling for future jobs and not hold desperately to 20th century tools and models.

On processes; the processes we use are antiquated and usually one war behind. I went to war in Afghanistan the first time based on AirLand battle doctrine, a doctrine designed for the cold war. That doctrine was still being trained right up until 2006 (five years into the war) when Generals Petraeus and Mattis came out with the counterinsurgency doctrine. We can and must do better.

Why did it take us nearly five years to change our doctrine when we were directly engaged in a counterinsurgency and counter terrorism campaign?

Bureaucracy and service parochial infighting are two of the answers.

Thank God our superb men and women, soldiers, sailors, airmen, marines and those civilians serving in combat innovate better than any other military in the world. When they realize that something is broken, they fix it on the battlefield instead of using the Pentagon's motto of, "If it's broke let somebody else fix it—we still need the money."

And lastly, the systems we have and the acquisition system that drives much of how our services and combatant commanders operate may as well be in separate solar systems and none of these (with few exceptions) seem to be anywhere near the battlefields we operate on today.

It is tempting to sit here and beat up those in the Pentagon and that would be unfair. But there are some in our system that see a jobs program, some who have never seen a program of record they didn't like, and some who abuse the system so badly, that it makes corrupt governments in Third World nations blush.

Additionally, after nearly fourteen years of war, conflict, call it what you will, we are engaged with enemies of our country and they want to win. I am not certain we have demonstrated the resilience or fortitude to do the same (at least not yet).

There are many in the defense system that have yet to experience that and do not understand the demands of combat and there are others who avoid it—wishing it will go away. It won't.

We (you) have to fix a number of things, but one of the most important is the acquisition system.

It must be joint and it must include the warfighter requirements and not simply serve the service chiefs and their constituent's needs.

Secretary Gates found this and fixed it, but to do so, he had to become the best action officer in the Pentagon.

That said, let me list a couple of ideas to consider as we go through the rest of this session and as you contemplate what steps to take to truly reform our system (all of which I will be ready to address in the Q&A).

1. Tooth-to-tail ratio must change (reverse it before we find ourselves not ready to fight never mind win)—we have way too much overhead and our staffs have become bloated beyond the nonsense stage.

2. Related to above, we have way too many four stars (commands and otherwise) around the world and too many four star headquarters in each of the services (11 "warfighting" commands alone). The service four and three star positions could easily be reduced a rank (or cut) and the staffs could subsequently be reduced.

3. Cut the civilian system in half or more. Turn those dollars into readiness and place more tooth into our warfighting forces. Be cautious about salami slicing, and help the SecDef and the senior civilian and military leaders make the best decisions based on a unified and strategic national security vision, approved by the president, instead of slicing to benefit some constituency—you must play a role but, very candidly, and over many years, congress created much of this mess and now you have an opportunity and a responsibility to correct it.

4. We need to seriously look at how we organize to fight and win in war. We man, train, and equip as services (i.e., Title 10), we go to war as a joint force (USAF carries the Army, Marines takes the Navy—in general), but we only win as a coalition—please name one time when we didn't fight as a coalition. We need to determine if we are creating a force that is not only technically qualified but also culturally and societally understanding and smart—language training for example is something that we need to place greater emphasis on for those officers serving in maneuver and operational assignments (foreign languages are not just for the Intelligence Community and attaches). For example, maybe we make it a prerequisite for combatant commanders to speak a foreign language before they can be even considered for a combatant command assignment. Maybe we do that for a majority of our three and four star assignments (that example would go a long way and reverberate across the entire force).

5. Significantly increase the tenure and the stature of the Chairman of the Joint Chiefs of Staff and the Vice Chairman. Tenures with a minimum of five years (without reconfirmation) should be considered. Why five years? In order to last longer than the service chiefs and potentially serve or overlap two presidents. This maintains the unbiased responsibility the CJCS (and the VCJCS when required) has as the principal military advisor to the POTUS.

6. Conduct a thorough and comprehensive overhaul of the defense acquisition system. Look at every single program of record. Every program not currently meeting its timelines or budgets should be immediately cut. No questions. Send a message that waste and substandard performance will no longer be tolerated—that would send shock waves through the system, would be nearly impossible to do—but it would be the harder right thing to do—I don't believe you could do it, but it would be interesting to see how many programs are actually up to standard—very few in my experience and my judgment.

7. Increase the investment in small businesses. Today, I believe the Defense Department policy states a goal of 25 percent investments in small businesses across the Department. Small businesses are the engine of change in our country and with the rapid advancements in technologies across the board (from healthcare to intelligence), we must seek new, innovative (and disruptive) ways to force fundamental change. Most on this committee would be challenged to recognize the Fortune 100 never mind Fortune 500. They are all relatively new and many started as small businesses in the last decade. As stated, small businesses also innovate. They have to, in order to survive. My strongest suggestion for consideration only at this stage is to increase the small business investment goals of the Department to fifty percent. I believe the Department and, especially our warfighters, would benefit most, and many would benefit overnight. Lastly, small businesses are the best way to increase our nation's economic strength. They will help us retool our nation for the digital age.

8. Decide who and where decisions about acquisition reform can be made. The SecDef cannot make them all. But if a service chief comes in and says we need this program (can't live without it) and a combatant commander comes in and says that program isn't working, then don't let the system decide to keep it and fix it on the margins or edges. Get rid of it. If they see something elsewhere and that is the capability they want (especially our warfighting commanders) and it can be procured in the requisite amounts within existing budgets get it to them rapidly or allow them to acquire it without going through the morass of bureaucracy. Secretary Gates experienced this first hand with ISR, medevac, and MRAPs to name a few. Again, he became the top action officer in the Pentagon because the people involved and the system itself were simply too slow, too bureaucratic and we were losing two wars. Amazing how,

at that time, no one but the SecDef inside of the Pentagon, at senior leader levels, could see that—why?

In this context, the questions this committee is considering are, in my judgment, the correct ones: namely, whether our nation's institutions of national defense are organized, manned, equipped, and managed in ways that can deal with the security challenges of the 21st century and that efficiently and effectively spend defense dollars.

The Department is not meeting those challenges today. We are not ready to deal with the challenges we, as the global leader, with the premier military capability on the planet, should be capable of in the future.

Without fundamental and massive reform as well as some smart, numerous, and targeted reductions in areas that have grown bloated, irrelevant and useless, we could find ourselves on the losing end of a major war—one that sitting here today we are unable to predict.

If our nation is proud of being the world's leader, let's start acting like it, and as our very first president stated, ''To be prepared for war is one of the most effective means of preserving peace.''

Thank you for this opportunity and I look forward to answering your questions.

Chairman McCAIN. Thank you, General.

General Jones?

STATEMENT OF GENERAL JAMES L. JONES, USMC, RETIRED, FORMER NATIONAL SECURITY ADVISOR TO THE PRESIDENT OF THE UNITED STATES; SUPREME ALLIED COMMANDER, EUROPE AND COMMANDER OF U.S. EUROPEAN COMMAND; AND 32ND COMMANDANT OF THE MARINE CORPS

Mr. JONES. Well, thank you, Mr. Chairman, Senator Reed, members of the committee. Thank you for inviting me to add to the expert testimony that you have already received from many other witnesses. I am honored to be here with my colleagues, General Flynn and Secretary Donley, to add my own views.

But before I start, may I also thank the committee for section 1227 of the NDAA [The National Defense Authorization Act] that was recently passed, which pledges that the United States will do more to protect the residents of Camp Liberty who have since my last testimony been attacked and lost over 20 lives and multiple injuries with very little global interest on their fate. There are 2,000 people sitting there, trapped, and we need to get them out of there. But I thank the committee very much for your support.

Mr. Chairman, I too would like to commend the committee for its leadership in undertaking this Goldwater-Nichols analysis concerning what changes might be necessary in our security architecture based on today's new and swiftly evolving environment.

I have a full statement, but I will summarize it as briefly as I can.

At the outset, let me say that I wish to identify myself fully with the testimonies previously offered by Mr. Jim Locher, Major General Punaro, and Dr. John Hamre and likewise Secretary Donley here today and General Flynn. Most of the people I just mentioned were among those who throughout their distinguished careers contributed significantly to the passage and implementation of Goldwater-Nichols in 1986. So it is not my intent to repeat their testimonies phrased in different words, but rather I hope to be of service to the committee and its work by focusing on just a few points gathered from the experience of my serving in senior military positions and as National Security Advisor.

Until this committee's current efforts, the most comprehensive review of Goldwater-Nichols and its so-called unintended consequences across the Department was commissioned in 1997 by then Secretary of Defense Bill Cohen when I served as his military assistant. While 18 years old now, in my view that study still stands in my opinion as the best effort to date in identifying necessary Goldwater-Nichols impacts and reforms, and I highly recommend that this committee revisit the task force's findings as you undertake the task of modernizing the Defense Department and our military forces to face 21st century challenges.

In the course of the important work the committee is undertaking, we should remember distinctly that the Senate passed the original Goldwater-Nichols Act by a vote of 95 to nothing. This overwhelming consensus was achieved despite the strong objections from the Department of Defense civilian and military leadership of the time. This clearly suggests to me that any future revision of Goldwater-Nichols should again be undertaken objectively and externally to the Department of Defense for three reasons.

One, the Department is consumed with everyday problems around the globe of increasing complexity.

Two, moreover large bureaucracies have inherent difficulty in implementing change from within.

Lastly, as we all know, reform challenges and entrenched interests will fiercely resist many of the recommendations proposed by our previous witnesses and perhaps my own included.

So my full statement focuses on four areas that I believe should be part of any effort to produce a Goldwater-Nichols II to improve our national security.

The first is fixing the overwhelming and unsustainable ''all in'' personnel costs for the all-volunteer force in addressing the systemic imbalances that endanger the Department's capacities and capabilities.

Second, to reform the appallingly wasteful and inefficient DOD business model for operations.

Three, moving towards a new interagency balance centers around unified commands.

Four, modernizing the roles, missions, and organizations of the National Security Council. That last point was not in the original Goldwater-Nichols, but in view of the importance of the National Security Council, I think that it should be part of any consideration of a Goldwater-Nichols II.

So with regard to personnel costs, the past three Secretaries of Defense, Secretaries Gates, Panetta, and Hagel, have each publicly stated that the cost growth of personnel expenditures in general is unsustainable. The cost growth in military pay, quality of life, retired pay, and VA [Veterans Affairs] and DOD health care costs far exceed both the GDP [Gross Domestic Product] and the Employment Cost Index.

Interim report of the Military Compensation and Retirement Modernization Commission stated that there was a $1 trillion unfunded liability over the next 10 years in military retirement that is not in any budget.

The current Commandant, General Robert Neller, is challenged, for example, by the reality of having to spend approximately 68 percent of his budget on those same costs. By comparison, 12 years ago when I was in the similar job as Commandant of the Marine Corps in 2003, my expenditure for those same costs was approximately 49 percent. So you have a significant cost growth over 12 years, and left unchanged, 10 years from now or 12 years from now, our budget will be increasingly consumed by personnel costs. This disturbing trend will accelerate and will weaken the armed forces' capabilities to fulfill their roles and missions.

The remedy is to modernize the pay and benefits for the active duty, reserve, DOD civilian, and retired communities and reform a system built for a different force in a bygone era featuring numerous anachronisms, as noted in my full statement.

In fairness for all who served on today's active or reserve duty, the terms under which they entered active duty service should be honored before making any reforms that would affect the total force. I think billions of dollars could be saved by keeping the faith with our service members and those who enter service the day after the legislation is passed.

Resources once allocated to recruiting, training, and equipping front line forces are now being reallocated to support the increasingly top heavy headquarters components or, put another way, the tooth-to-tail ratio is spiraling out of control. The stifling bureaucracy yielded processes and procedures that are far too complex to perform once simple tasks. This dynamic has produced a paralyzing environment in which micro-management and endless consensus building impede initiative and impede action.

$113 billion to support 240,000 members of OSD, Joint Staff, and DOD headquarters illustrates the point. In 1958, the Joint Staff was authorized 400 personnel. Today the Joint Staff directorates have 4,000. Medical treatment facilities that are now being used at a 50 percent utilization rate but have a division's worth of medical administrators are still allocated $41.7 billion.

The enlarging tail is largely responsible for a broken acquisition system. Examples in each of the services. The Air Force's F–35 program, the Marine Corps' ill-fated AAAV [Advanced Amphibious Assault Vehicle] program, the Navy's *Ford*-class carrier program, the Army's Future Combat System. May I thank the committee also for your support in putting service chiefs back in the acquisition process. I think this is something that was long overdue and something that was an incredible frustration during my time as service chief.

Point number two was reforming wasteful, inefficient DOD business operations. DOD's agencies, once relevant and once perhaps a good idea—many have outlived their usefulness and they contribute little to our warfighting capabilities at huge, enormous expense, as General Flynn just referred to. They have avoided serious but needed reforms. The DOD agencies themselves consume 20 percent of the Defense Department's budgets.

As General Punaro testified, DOD's top two clients are DLA [the Defense Logistics Agency], which consumes $44.1 billion, and the second is the defense health programs, $41.7 billion. Number three is Lockheed Martin Corporation, $13.5 billion behind the top two DOD agencies at $28.2 billion.

I experienced significant frustration in dealing with agencies as a service chief back in 1999 to 2003, and listed in my detailed report is the story of how the Marine Corps changed its combat uniform and modernized it. Essentially I discovered in negotiating with DLA that my service would be assessed a 22 percent carrying charge for the service of going out and buying the uniform, and I politely declined, formed a small group of marines. We went out and did it ourselves at a cost far cheaper, far quicker, and more efficiently than anything DLA could do.

One question that I have frequently wondered is why are flag and general officers running businesses instead of commanding troops. Business-intensive defense agencies headed by active duty flag and general officers do not make a lot of sense to me. We need business experience to ensure fiscal solvency of agencies. We should staff these agencies with business executives and return military personnel to operational ranks to reduce the tooth-to-tail ratio that is spiraling out of control.

The tenth largest client of the Department of Defense is the Defense Commissary Agency, which is subsidized to the tune of $1.4 billion annually. What is the remedy? Outsource it. Walmart and other agencies like it can compete for the same job that the Defense Commissary Agencies are doing on our base at reduced cost to the taxpayer, lower inventory, transportation costs, without any subsidies, and higher potential savings for military families. In 2001, I volunteered my service as an experiment to test this, and it was soundly rejected as a result of the entrenched bureaucracies and the fact that I ran out of time as service chief and could not get it done.

Rebalancing the interagency and unified commands to meet 21st century threats is my third point. AFRICOM [United States Africa Command] is a good example of what I am about to talk about.

AFRICOM was created out of EUCOM. It was proposed by General Wald and myself, recognizing that Africa as a continent had arrived as a 21st century reality that needed to be recognized. Ironically, although most of Africa except for the Horn, was tasked to EUCOM, the word 'Africa' does not appear in the EUCOM title. We proposed AFRICOM in order to change that span of control which was much too big for one commander of Europe and Africa totaling some 85 countries.

But the value of unified commands fosters military interoperability, training, common military architectures, and requisite support to our friends and allies. They are extremely important. They are a gift of the 20th century. But they need to be changed to recognize the realities of the 21st century.

In my view, ideally unified commands should be in the geographical areas they purport to affect and to work in. We have taken some steps back over the years, but if I could change any one thing, I would place CENTCOM [United States Central Command], the Central Command, in its AOR [area of responsibility] as opposed to just a forward command, and I would, as I proposed to Secretary Rumsfeld, place AFRICOM in Africa where it would do the most good.

Absence of military unified commands in the regions creates vacuums. Vacuums are filled by people who do not have our interests, and routinely as I travel around the African continent, I am asked why is the U.S. not here. Why are we not more involved?

Why are we not competing with China more successfully? We need America. We want America.

The presence of U.S. companies, NGOs [non-governmental organizations], academic institutions, in a combined unified command headquarters would send powerful messages to that continent's 54 countries. The whole-of-government approach to 21st century engagement would show the U.S. as an enduring partner for all African nations seeking freedom and prosperity.

With your permission, Mr. Chairman, I would like to submit for the record a study called 'All Elements of National Power: Moving Toward a New Agency Balance for the U.S. Global Engagement,' prepared under the auspices of the Brent Scowcroft Center at the Atlantic Council, which I was privileged to chair.

Chairman McCAIN. Without objection.

[The information follows:]

All Elements of National Power

Moving Toward a New Interagency
Balance for US Global Engagement

Atlantic Council Combatant Command Task Force
Task Force Chairman: Gen. James L. Jones, Jr., USMC (Ret.)
Project Rapporteur: Lt. Col. Kim Campbell, USAF

All Elements of National Power
Moving Toward a New Interagency Balance for US Global Engagement

Atlantic Council Combatant Command Task Force
Task Force Chairman: Gen. James L. Jones, Jr., USMC (Ret.)
Project Rapporteur: Lt. Col. Kim Campbell, USAF

Atlantic Council
1030 15th Street, NW, 12th Floor
Washington, DC 20005

ISBN: 978-1-61977-063-8

July 2014

ABOUT THE ATLANTIC COUNCIL
COMBATANT COMMAND TASK FORCE

The Brent Scowcroft Center on International Security at the Atlantic Council convened a task force to conduct analysis and to make actionable recommendations regarding a transformed regional interagency balance better suited for engaging with key allies and partners to improve foreign and defense policy execution and advance US interests at the regional level. Chaired by former National Security Advisor General James Jones, the task force was comprised of former senior US government officials, both from the Department of Defense and Department of State, as well as respected thought leaders and experts. The members of the task force helped shape the report's scope, findings, and recommendations but do not necessarily agree with all of its conclusions or recommendations.

TASK FORCE MEMBERS

Ambassador Lawrence Butler (Ret.)*
Former EUCOM Civilian Deputy to the Commander and Foreign Policy Adviser, 2011-13
Former Political Adviser to the Commanding General, US Forces - Iraq, 2010-11
Former Political Adviser to NATO's Supreme Allied Commander Europe, 2008-10

Vice Admiral Kevin Cosgriff, USN (Ret.)*
Former Commander, US Naval Forces Central Command, 2007-08

General John Craddock, USA (Ret.)**
Strategic Global Adviser
Engility Corporation
Former Supreme Allied Commander Europe and EUCOM Commander, 2006-09
Former SOUTHCOM Commander, 2004-06

General Douglas Fraser, USAF (Ret.)
Principal
Doug Fraser LLC
Former SOUTHCOM Commander, 2009-12
Former PACOM Deputy Commander, 2008-09

Mr. James Hasik
Nonresident Senior Fellow, Brent Scowcroft Center on International Security
Atlantic Council

General James L. Jones, Jr., USMC (Ret.)**
Chairman, Brent Scowcroft Center on International Security
Atlantic Council
Former National Security Advisor, 2009-10
Former Supreme Allied Commander Europe and EUCOM Commander, 2003-06
Former Commandant of the Marine Corps, 1999-2003

Ambassador George Moose (Ret.)**
Vice Chairman, Board of Directors
United States Institute of Peace
Former US Permanent Representative to the European Office of the United Nations, 1998-2001
Former Assistant Secretary of State for African Affairs, 1993-97

Mr. Vago Muradian*
Editor
Defense News

Mr. Barry Pavel
Vice President and Director, Brent Scowcroft Center on International Security
Atlantic Council
Former Special Assistant to the President, Senior Director for Defense Policy & Strategy, National Security Council staff, 2008-10

General Gene Renuart, USAF (Ret.)
President
The Renuart Group LLC
Former NORTHCOM Commander, 2007-10

Mr. Russell Rumbaugh
Director, Budgeting for Foreign Affairs and Defense and Senior Associate
The Stimson Center

Dr. Harvey Sapolsky
Professor of Public Policy and Organization, Emeritus
Massachusetts Institute of Technology

General Norton Schwartz, USAF (Ret.)
President and CEO
Business Executives for National Security
Former Chief of Staff of the Air Force, 2008-12
Former TRANSCOM Commander, 2005-08

Mr. David Sedney
Former Deputy Assistant Secretary of Defense for Afghanistan, Pakistan, and Central Asia, 2009-13

Mr. Andrew Shapiro
Managing Director
Beacon Global Strategies
Former US Assistant Secretary of State for Political-Military Affairs, 2009-13

Mr. Stephen Shapiro*
Managing Partner
BSR Investments

Mr. Walter Slocombe**
Senior Counsel
Caplin & Drysdale
Former Under Secretary of Defense for Policy, 1994-2001

Mr. Harlan Ullman
Senior Adviser
Atlantic Council
Advisory board member for the Supreme Allied Commander Europe

Dr. Cynthia Watson
Professor of Strategy
National Defense University

Ambassador Mary Yates (Ret.)**
Former Special Assistant to the President, Senior Director for African Affairs, National Security Council staff, 2009-2011
Former AFRICOM Deputy to the Commander for Civil-Military Activities, 2007-09
Former EUCOM Foreign Policy Adviser, 2005-07

Dr. Dov S. Zakheim**
Senior Adviser
Center for Strategic and International Studies
Former Under Secretary of Defense (Comptroller), 2001-04

TASK FORCE INTERVIEWS

General James Cartwright, USMC (Ret.)**
Harold Brown Chair in Defense Policy Studies
Center for Strategic and International Studies
Former Vice Chairman of the Joint Chiefs of Staff, 2007-11
Former STRATCOM Commander, 2004-07

General Carter Ham, USA (Ret.)
Former AFRICOM Commander, 2011-13
Former Commander, US Army Europe, 2008-11

Ambassador Ryan Crocker (Ret.)
Dean and Executive Professor
The George Bush School of Government and Public
Service, Texas A&M University
Former US Ambassador to Afghanistan, 2011-12
Former US Ambassador to Iraq, 2007-09
Former US Ambassador to Pakistan, 2004-07

Mr. Stephen Hadley**
Principal
RiceHadleyGates LLC
Former National Security Advisor, 2005-09

Ambassador Zalmay Khalilzad (Ret.)**
President
Gryphon Partners
*Former US Permanent Representative to the United
Nations, 2007-09*
Former US Ambassador to Iraq, 2005-07
Former US Ambassador to Afghanistan, 2003-05

General Peter Pace, USMC (Ret.)*
Operating Partner
Behrman Capital
Former Chairman of the Joint Chiefs of Staff, 2005-07
Former Vice Chairman of the Joint Chiefs of Staff, 2001-05
Former SOUTHCOM Commander, 2000-01

Ambassador James Smith (Ret.)
Senior Counselor
The Cohen Group
Former US Ambassador to Saudi Arabia, 2009-13

Admiral James Stavridis, USN (Ret.)**
Dean
The Fletcher School, Tufts University
*Former Supreme Allied Commander Europe and EUCOM
Commander, 2009-13*
Former SOUTHCOM Commander, 2006-09

General Anthony Zinni, USMC (Ret.)
Former CENTCOM Commander, 1997-2000

* Atlantic Council Member

** Atlantic Council Board Director

FOREWORD

The United States faces a dynamic and unsettled global security environment that promises to remain with us far into the twenty-first century. Emerging powers, regional instability, individual empowerment, and political turbulence will continue to present the US national security community with new challenges. Yet this environment also offers new opportunities to leverage American strengths to advance our interests and values abroad. In light of this evolving strategic context, the United States must adjust how it engages internationally to foster a more holistic and whole-of-government approach to national security policy.

The US geographic combatant commands are priceless in strategic value, but their structure, function, and organization are increasingly relics of a bygone era. A purely military approach to the myriad of national security challenges that the nation faces will no longer be enough. Indeed, this is one of the key strategic lessons learned from the campaigns in Iraq and Afghanistan. Now is the time to act on these lessons to provide options for a whole-of-government approach to US national security policy that leverages all tools of American power and statecraft. The United States must move forward with a synchronized and coordinated interagency approach from initial planning to execution in order to confront the vast array of challenges and threats in the twenty-first century.

I believe this report provides new analysis and key insights into the issues associated with rebalancing our national instruments of power. Some of the findings and recommendations may be controversial and unorthodox, but I believe they are necessary. Indeed, unconventional thinking is required if the United States is to properly adapt to an unconventional strategic landscape.

I would like to offer a special thanks to project rapporteur, US Air Force Fellow Lt. Col. Kim Campbell, and all of those on the task force who lent their time, talents, and expertise to the project. I commend the Atlantic Council for launching this important study at a critical time in history.

James L Jones

Gen. James L. Jones, Jr., USMC (Ret.)
Chairman, Brent Scowcroft Center on International Security
Atlantic Council

EXECUTIVE SUMMARY

To deal effectively with long-range global trends and near-term security challenges, the United States requires a broader application of all elements of national power or risks continued disjointed efforts in US global engagement. A transformed interagency balance is a hedge against uncertainty in a dramatically changing world.

As the US National Intelligence Council suggested in its landmark 2012 report, *Global Trends 2030: Alternative Worlds*, tectonic shifts in several theaters will have significant potential to cause global and regional insecurity in the coming decades. American overseas presence in key regions is and will remain integral to meeting dynamic regional security challenges and specific military threats. The United States faces increased risks and missed opportunities to advance US interests, however, if it continues to focus on the military as the primary government instrument working with allies and partners on a regional scale. The US government currently has only one structure, the geographic combatant command, to execute foreign and defense policy in key regions of the world. At present, there is no mechanism in place to integrate activities of all US government departments and agencies in key regions.

As a result, US government regional actions often are uncoordinated and disconnected. To this end, recent geographic combatant commanders have recognized the need for greater interagency coordination and experimented with strengthening the role and relevance of the interagency within their commands. The intent of this report is to go further and make interagency components the key integrator of elements of national power to better manage foreign and defense policy execution. This report discusses how the United States can resource and restructure for a more balanced, forward-deployed regional approach essential in improving the integration of national instruments of power–diplomatic, informational, military, economic, and others–to advance US interests at the regional level. This task force initially focused solely on restructuring the geographic combatant commands, but it quickly became apparent that higher-priority, untapped points of leverage existed that, if properly resourced, could greatly strengthen US efforts at the regional level. Although these general recommendations are Department of Defense- and Department of State-centric, we recognize the importance for all US government agencies and departments to play a role in a true "whole-of-government" approach. Initial discussion focuses primarily on security issues with the goal of bringing in the full range of economic, political, and other issues and agencies as changes progress. Many of the recommendations could be implemented in the near- to mid-term under the current structures of the Department of State and the Department of Defense. The following general recommendations were developed toward that end:

Interagency synchronization

- The United States should rebalance national instruments of power by providing enhanced Department of State capacity in key regions. Unbalanced resourcing and manpower between the Department of Defense and the Department of State creates significant roadblocks to enhancing interagency presence in the region. A more balanced approach would strengthen US engagement more broadly.

- Department of State regional assistant secretaries should be further empowered to set and coordinate foreign policy within the regions. Currently, assistant secretaries have an explicit requirement to be responsible, but they lack sufficient resources and authority to be effective. Regional assistant secretaries should have the authority to integrate the full range of foreign and security policy as well as diplomatic resources to execute foreign policy on a regional scale.

- There should be an ambassador-level civilian deputy in each geographic combatant command with deep regional experience and expertise. Absent crisis or war, the civilian deputy would, on behalf of the commander, oversee and integrate security cooperation efforts with allies and partners. The civilian deputy could also act as the senior political adviser (POLAD) who would have direct liaison with the Department of State regional assistant secretary. Likewise, the senior political-military advisers in the Department of State regional bureaus should have direct "reach-forward" access to applicable geographic combatant command leadership as well as a direct link to civilian deputies/senior POLADs in the geographic combatant commands. If the civilian deputy and senior POLAD are two different positions (depending on combatant command structure), then the civilian deputy would serve as the senior-most civilian representative within the combatant command and the primary link to the Department of State. The senior POLAD would act as the policy adviser to the combatant commander.

- To reach the fullest potential and ensure sustained, effective change, interagency legislation to support these changes would be essential, entailing provisions that would direct departments and agencies to adopt a whole-of-government approach. Legislation could use the Goldwater-Nichols Department of Defense Reorganization Act of 1986 as a model.

Organizational transformation

- Geographic combatant commands should be renamed to signify the importance of a whole-of-government approach. A name change to "unified regional commands" would reinforce efforts to coordinate and integrate instruments for foreign and defense policy execution and would represent broader capabilities and engagement efforts than strictly a war-fighting approach.

- Allies and partners could play a more significant role in geographic combatant commands; international involvement could strengthen allied/partner nation support for US policies and improve prepositioning and posture opportunities.

- Geographic combatant commanders should be assigned for sufficient time (at least three or four years versus two or three years at present) to gain a deeper understanding of the region and help fortify relations with regional counterparts.

- Divergence of regional boundaries among the Department of Defense, Department of State, and National Security Council causes friction and confusion; a common "map" would enhance a whole-of-government approach.

Efficiencies

- Certain regionally prepositioned supplies and equipment should be managed in a more coordinated manner by departments and agencies. Integrated prepositioning would save money and manpower, eliminate redundancies, and provide for a synchronized approach to crisis response resulting in quicker reaction times.

- Major efficiencies can be gained by returning "back office" functions from the geographic combatant commands and their service component commands to the Services and the Joint Staff, thereby streamlining geographic combatant command headquarters staffs. The secretary of defense and chairman of the Joint Chiefs of Staff should request a qualified outside group to assess details and report back in sixty to ninety days.

The task force also evaluated three specific restructuring options that would help move US regional presence toward a more effective interagency balance. Although these restructuring options require legislative and organizational changes and are a move away from long-standing institutional norms, they are worthy of discussion and should be evaluated based on emerging twenty-first century strategic and fiscal realities. The following restructuring options should be explored:

1. An unconventional end-state would be the creation of an "Interagency Regional Center" that would act as a regional interagency headquarters for foreign and defense policy. This new organization would result in the unification of the Department of Defense and the Department of State (as well as other agencies and departments) at the regional level. The Interagency Regional Center (IRC) would be led by an "interagency regional director" with regional experience and expertise who would report directly to the president or vice president of the United States. The president develops the grand strategy and establishes national security strategy, while the regional directors would implement that strategy at the regional level. The regional directors would advise and participate in the National Security Council as requested. Regional directors would also convene to discuss cross-regional issues and activities. The IRCs would ensure long-lasting integration of all instruments of national power.

   The interagency regional director would have a military and civilian deputy. The military deputy would focus on defense issues while the civilian deputy would focus on diplomacy, development, and other critical nonmilitary issues. The civilian deputy would also act as a regional ambassador-at-large who would have coordination authority for country ambassadors and other civilian-led organizations such as Treasury, Justice, and Commerce. Country ambassadors would still formally report directly to the Secretary of State through the IRC. The civilian deputy would be in charge of coordinating all nonmilitary agencies and organizations at the regional level. During wartime, the military commander would report directly to the president through the secretary of defense as in the current combatant command structure, while the director and civilian deputy would focus on nation-building and postconflict operations. During peacetime, the military would report through the IRC for engagement. For this approach to be successful, peacetime and wartime responsibilities would need to be clearly delineated and understood.

2. An intermediate approach would colocate the Department of State regional bureaus with the geographic combatant commands. These locations would be ideal to strengthen the authority of regional bureaus and allow the bureaus to operate more nimbly. Colocation of the regional assistant secretary (or alternatively, a deputy assistant secretary) and his/her staff with the geographic combatant command would allow for regional-level integration with a more unified approach and presence. Colocation of other departments and agencies, such as Central Intelligence Agency (CIA) regional offices, should also be considered.

3. An alternative intermediate approach would be for the geographic combatant command civilian deputy to act also as a regional ambassador-at-large who would have coordination authority for country ambassadors and other civilian-led organizations in the region. His/her mission under this authority would be to coordinate US actions, issues, and initiatives within the region and bordering regions. The civilian deputy would have the authority to require consultation between regional organizations, but would not have the authority to compel agreement. This coordination authority would be a consultation relationship, not an authority through which chain of command would be exercised. This approach works under the current structure, but adds integration by bringing together all agencies operating within the region to coordinate regional activities.

It is critical that the United States think about how to adapt to emerging twenty-first-century realities, both strategic and fiscal, particularly as the United States transitions from a decade at war. Long-range global trends and near-term security challenges demand a broader use of instruments of national power. The United States must take advantage of its strategic assets, and resource and restructure for a better balanced, forward deployed approach. The secretary of defense, chairman of the Joint Chiefs of Staff, the secretary of state, and the national security advisor should commission a detailed follow-on study to this report to further evaluate key insights and execution of suggested recommendations.

TABLE OF CONTENTS

41

STRATEGIC CONTEXT

To deal effectively with long-range global trends and near-term security challenges, the United States requires a broader application of all elements of national power or risks disjointed efforts in US global engagement. A transformed interagency balance is a hedge against uncertainty in a dramatically changing world.

As the US National Intelligence Council suggested in its landmark 2012 report, *Global Trends 2030: Alternative Worlds*, tectonic shifts in several theaters will have significant potential to cause global and regional insecurity in the coming decades.[1] A regional strategy is fundamental in dealing with these issues, and it is essential that the United States better integrate the national instruments of power—diplomatic, informational, military, economic, and others—to advance US interests at the regional level. A transformed regional interagency balance will help mitigate risks while ensuring a strategy-driven US government approach for foreign and defense policy execution that reassures friends and allies and reinforces US commitment to key regions.

> IT IS ESSENTIAL THAT THE UNITED STATES BETTER INTEGRATE THE NATIONAL INSTRUMENTS OF POWER—DIPLOMATIC, INFORMATIONAL, MILITARY, ECONOMIC, AND OTHERS—TO ADVANCE US INTERESTS AT THE REGIONAL LEVEL.

It is impractical to tackle many current and future challenges without approaching them from a regional perspective. Country-by-country execution of foreign policy by US ambassadors may not always be the most effective or successful approach. For example, water supply, food distribution, and security all require a regional outlook especially with increasing competition for scarce resources, the growing likelihood of large-scale natural disasters, and the propensity for intensifying regional conflicts. Overall execution of

foreign policy can be improved upon by having regional policy development and execution guided by regional execution agencies. At this time, the United States has only one government structure, the geographic combatant command, for execution of foreign and defense policy at the regional level. The United States will face increased risks and missed opportunities to advance US interests if it focuses mainly on a military approach at the regional level. There is currently no mechanism in place to integrate activities of all US government departments and agencies in key regions.

As a result, US government regional actions often are uncoordinated and disconnected. To this end, recent combatant commanders have recognized the need for greater interagency coordination and have experimented in strengthening the role and relevance of the interagency within their commands. The intent of this report is to go further and make interagency components the key integrator of elements of national power to better manage foreign and defense policy execution. This report will discuss how the United States can better take advantage of its strategic assets, and resource and restructure for a more balanced, forward-deployed regional approach.

Both the Department of State and the Department of Defense have recognized the need for greater coordination and collaboration in the execution of national security policy. The 2010 Quadrennial Diplomacy and Development Review stated: "Development, diplomacy, and defense, as the core pillars of American foreign policy, must mutually reinforce and complement one another in an integrated, comprehensive approach to national security."[2] The 2014 Quadrennial Defense Review (QDR) stated that "the Department is committed to finding creative, effective, and efficient ways to achieve our goals and assist in making strategic choices. Innovation—within our own Department and in our interagency and international partnerships—is a central line of effort."[3] Furthermore, Secretary of Defense Chuck Hagel's speech at the Munich Security Conference in February 2014 outlined the need to restore "balance to the relationship between American defense and diplomacy."[4]

1 US National Intelligence Council, *Global Trends 2030: Alternative Worlds*, http://www.dni.gov/files/documents/GlobalTrends_2030.pdf.

2 Department of State, *Quadrennial Diplomacy and Development Review: Leading through Civilian Power*, http://www.state.gov/s/dmr/qddr/.

3 Department of Defense, *Quadrennial Defense Review 2014*, http://www.defense.gov/pubs/2014_Quadrennial_Defense_Review.pdf.

4 Secretary of Defense, *Munich Security Conference*, http://www.defense.gov/Speeches/Speech.aspx?SpeechID=1828.

All Elements of National Power

US Navy forces unload supplies during 2010 earthquake relief efforts in Port-au-Prince, Haiti. Photo credit: Petty Officer 2nd Class Daniel Barker, USN.

This report examines how geographic combatant commands could be internally realigned to meet new circumstances and engagement requirements and to better integrate interagency tools for foreign and defense policy execution in key regions. This report will also offer general recommendations that will help the United States move toward a regional interagency balance for engaging with key allies and partners that would advance US interests on a regional scale. It is critical that the United States think about how to adapt to emerging twenty-first century realities, both strategic and fiscal, particularly as the United States transitions from a decade at war.

As it ends its sustained combat role in the wars in Iraq and Afghanistan, the United States needs to ensure that it captures critical lessons learned and best practices from interagency successes and failures. Wartime experience has proven that interagency integration is critical to successful operations. Although the initial stages of Iraq and Afghanistan prioritized military operations, reconstruction, stability efforts, and political developments necessarily blurred the lines between military force and diplomacy due to a challenging and unsettled environment. Military and civilian officials were forced to work together and learned hard lessons regarding interagency collaboration and coordination. It is imperative that these lessons be formalized and used in peacetime efforts so that the US government does not have to reinvent the wheel as new crises emerge.

An effective interagency process that achieves unity of effort is absolutely essential to executing foreign and defense policy and advancing US interests now and in the future. A coordinated, integrated, and synchronized interagency plan could have ensured that the United States was prepared to address humanitarian assistance, governance, rule of law, and economic issues that emerged in Iraq and Afghanistan. Unfortunately, up to this point, many attempts at transforming the interagency process have not reached their full potential due to structural weaknesses in the interagency process as well as a lack of personnel, training, doctrine, and-most importantly-a forcing function to make them work in peacetime.

The opportunity for significant, effective change for interagency coordination and balance is greater now than ever before: the US military's role in the wars in Iraq and Afghanistan is coming to a close; the Department of Defense recently completed the QDR that affirmed that innovation within the interagency is a central line of effort; the president made a strategic decision to increase focus on the Asia-Pacific region and rebalance US engagements, activities, and resources toward and within the region; and the administration is in its final term where enough current administration officials understand the need for real change. As all of these factors converge, it is prudent to have an open discussion of how a transformed regional interagency balance for global engagement could help the United States meet the challenges of the twenty-first century.

PRINCIPLES AND ASSUMPTIONS

Regional overseas presence remains integral to meeting dynamic challenges and emerging threats in the twenty-first century. Security challenges such as terrorism, proliferation, and international criminal networks all require a more effective US government regional presence. Furthermore, the challenges presented by a rising China, the reemergence of a revanchist Russia, and terrorism/extremism in the Mideast and Africa also give credence to establishing a strong posture in key regions. For better or for worse, geographic combatant commands are currently the best resourced and most visible manifestations of US national power and interests in key overseas regions. With adequate resources, the Department of Defense can help manage risks and meet challenges (including those arising from reduced force structure) by employing the existing geographic combatant commands as assurance tools to mitigate regional concerns and advance US interests.

> REGIONAL OVERSEAS PRESENCE REMAINS INTEGRAL TO MEETING DYNAMIC CHALLENGES AND EMERGING THREATS IN THE TWENTY-FIRST CENTURY.

Geographic combatant commands allow the global presence and reach necessary to protect and advance US interests in key overseas regions. To improve efficiency and effectiveness of foreign and defense policy execution and advance US interests on a regional scale, however, the geographic combatant commands could be internally reorganized and augmented to meet new circumstances and engagement requirements within a whole-of-government approach. Former Secretary of State Hillary Clinton stated that "defense, diplomacy and development were not separate entities, either in substance or process, but that indeed they had to be viewed as part of an integrated whole and that the whole of government then had to be enlisted in their pursuit."[5] The Department of Defense defines whole-of-government as an approach that "integrates the collaborative efforts of the departments and agencies of the USG [United States government] to achieve unity of effort. Under unified action, a whole-of-government approach identifies combinations of the full range of available USG capabilities and resources that reinforce progress and create synergies."[6] If the geographic combatant commands are restructured toward this whole-of-government approach, then it is imperative that any restructuring must not detract from combatant commands' capabilities for executing their core warfighting functions and vital missions.

There are four primary core functions for geographic combatant commands:

- Geographic combatant commands must deter, detect, and help prevent attacks against the United States.

- When directed, geographic combatant commands will support and protect the interests of the United States.

- Geographic combatant commands must develop, coordinate, and implement theater engagement plans that support US interests and build partner nation capability and capacity.

- Geographic combatant commands must respond to natural disasters and humanitarian crises within authorities, means, and capabilities.

---

5 Jim Garamone, "New National Strategy Takes Whole-of-Government Approach," American Forces Press Service, May 27, 2010, http://www.defense.gov/news/newsarticle.aspx?id=59377.

6 Interorganizational Coordination during Joint Operations, Joint Publication 3-08 (Washington DC: The Joint Staff, 2004), p. xiii.

GENERAL RECOMMENDATIONS

This task force initially focused solely on restructuring the geographic combatant commands, but it quickly became apparent that higher-priority, untapped points of leverage existed that, if properly resourced, could greatly strengthen US efforts at the regional level. Although these general recommendations are Department of Defense- and Department of State-centric, we recognize the importance for all US government agencies and departments to play a role in a true "whole-of-government" approach. Initial discussion focuses primarily on security issues with the goal of bringing in the full range of economic, political, and environmental issues and agencies as changes progress. Many of the recommendations could be implemented in the near- to mid-term under the current internal structure of the Department of State and the Department of Defense. If implemented, these recommendations move toward a regional interagency balance, but still may fall short of fully executing a regional whole-of-government approach. The United States needs resources along with reorganization to compete effectively around the globe and to see a significant impact on foreign and defense policy execution.

Interagency synchronization

1. The United States should rebalance national instruments of power by providing enhanced Department of State capacity in key regions. Today, the United States faces increased risks and missed opportunities to advance US interests because it has focused on the military as the primary government instrument working with allies and partners at the regional level. As the United States ends its military role in the wars in Iraq and Afghanistan, it runs the risk of forgetting many of the lessons learned regarding the importance of a whole-of-government approach. Many of these critical wartime lessons and best practices also apply to peacetime and would improve US global engagement efforts with the ultimate goal of preventing future conflicts. The United States is at a key juncture where it can focus on these lessons and take action to formally implement changes; however, adequate resourcing is critical for greater synchronization among US government agencies. Specifically, unbalanced resourcing and manpower between the Department of Defense and the Department of State creates significant roadblocks to enhancing interagency presence in the region. A balanced approach would strengthen US engagement more broadly. Significant

congressional intervention and action is required to move forward with balanced resource options to ensure proper adjustment of budgets, manpower, equipment, training, missions, and responsibilities. Due to a challenging climate, it will require a unified Department of Defense/Department of State effort to begin to move forward with these changes.

2. Department of State regional assistant secretaries should be further empowered to set and coordinate the execution of foreign policy within the regions. Currently, assistant secretaries have an explicit requirement to be responsible, but they lack sufficient resources and authority to be effective. Regional assistant secretaries should have the authority to integrate the full range of foreign and defense policy as well as diplomatic resources to execute foreign policy on a regional scale. The United States needs to get ahead of future problems and reduce the seams that hamper foreign policy. To do this, the connection between the geographic combatant commands and the regional bureaus needs to be strengthened. The regional assistant secretaries need to be able to set the agenda in the region and have the ability to call on resources to implement the agenda. Providers, such as the US Agency for International Development (USAID), Drug Enforcement Agency, Federal Bureau of Investigation, and others would then have to align their resources with policy goals. A rewrite of regional assistant secretary job requirements is needed to explicitly establish their authority to be a counterpart to the geographic combatant commanders. For this recommendation to be successful, the Office of the Secretary of Defense would have to defer to the Department of State on broader policy formulation but would still retain policy oversight on geographic combatant command activities. The National Security Council would also have to concur and honor the empowerment of the regional assistant secretaries.

3. There should be an ambassador-level civilian deputy in each geographic combatant command with deep regional experience and expertise. Absent crisis or war, the civilian deputy would, on behalf of the commander, oversee and integrate security cooperation efforts with allies and partners. Currently, only three of the six geographic combatant commands have civilian deputy commanders. The civilian deputy would provide

PERSONNEL EXCHANGE—THE FIRST STEP

On January 4, 2012, the Department of State and the Department of Defense signed a memorandum of understanding that specified the terms and conditions under which certain personnel from one agency will be assigned on a nonreimbursable basis to the other agency. The memorandum of understanding further stipulated that "the DoD and DoS have a shared responsibility for national security and need to coordinate carefully on numerous issues affecting both foreign policy and defense. The long-standing practice of personnel exchanges between these two agencies has greatly facilitated this coordination. The exchange of personnel enhances the breadth of each agency's viewpoints, develops a strong cadre of political-military experts, and through the selection of good employees for exchange, makes substantive contributions to the work of both agencies."

civilian representation at the command level within all geographic combatant commands. The civilian deputy should be the senior diplomatic adviser and be able to act as a senior representative of the secretary of state.

The civilian deputy could also act as the senior POLAD who would have direct liaison with the Department of State regional assistant secretary. However, to be effective, it is imperative that the civilian deputy/POLAD be properly resourced and staffed. The senior POLAD should serve as the combatant command focal point on diplomatic issues for interaction with the National Security Council, Department of State, relevant US embassies, and foreign diplomatic missions in the region. The senior POLAD should also assist the command in developing political/diplomatic strategies and speak authoritatively for the command on relevant political issues to diplomatic counterparts.[7]

One of the central roles of the POLAD is to ensure that the US government speaks with one voice. POLADs are in a position to advise geographic combatant commanders on the command's action and activities being in accord with US foreign policy. Officially (per Annex A–Descriptions of Department of State positions at DoD, Memorandum of Understanding between the Department of Defense and the Department of State regarding Non-Reimbursable Exchange of Personnel), the POLAD reports directly to the commander and works closely with the deputy commander to provide advice and support on foreign policy issues of concern and relevance to the command.[8]

However, Annex A should also specify that the senior POLAD should have direct liaison with the Department of State regional assistant secretary to improve coordination and communication between the regional bureau and the geographic combatant command. Likewise, the senior political-military advisers in the Department of State regional bureaus should have direct "reach-forward" to applicable geographic combatant command leadership as well as a direct link to civilian deputy/senior POLADs in the geographic combatant commands.

If the civilian deputy and senior POLAD are two different positions, then the civilian deputy would be the senior most civilian representative within the combatant command and would be the primary link to the Department of State. The senior POLAD would act as the policy adviser to the combatant commander. These relationships and communication links should be explicitly defined in their roles and responsibilities. Ultimately, it is essential that both the Department of State and the Department of Defense are aware of and are leveraging the resources that currently exist.

4. To reach the fullest potential and ensure sustained, effective change, interagency legislation to support these changes would be essential. This interagency legislation would entail provisions that would direct departments and agencies to adopt a whole-of-government approach and think beyond organizational cultures and traditions. This legislation could use the Goldwater-Nichols Department of Defense Reorganization Act of 1986 that directed military services to work together achieving critical efficiencies and improved operability as a model.

Reforms for training and advancement should specifically be included in any interagency legislation. A 2009 Government Accountability Office (GAO) study on interagency collaboration reported that agencies' personnel systems do

---

7 European Command (EUCOM) job description for the civilian deputy to the commander, http://www.eucom.mil/organization/command-structure/civilian-deputy-to-the-commander-foreign-policy-advisor.

8 "Annex A – Descriptions of State Department Positions at DoD," Memorandum of Understanding between the Department of Defense and the Department of State regarding Non-reimbursable Exchange of Personnel, January 4, 2012.

All Elements of National Power

President Obama and Vice President Biden meet with combatant commanders and military leadership. Photo credit: Pete Souza, Official White House Photo.

not always facilitate interagency collaboration, with interagency assignments often not being considered as career enhancing or recognized in performance management systems.[9] Under interagency legislation, personnel submitted for interagency exchange or liaison positions should be among those considered the most outstanding of that agency. Additionally, in order for promotion and advancement, personnel would have to be designated as interagency qualified. Reforms such as these have ensured a highly capable joint force and can be carried over to the interagency environment to facilitate greater collaboration and professional development of US government personnel involved in national security.

Organizational transformation

1. Geographic combatant commands should be renamed to signify the importance of a whole-of-government approach. A name change to "unified regional command" would reinforce efforts to coordinate and integrate foreign and defense policy execution and would represent broader capabilities and engagement efforts than strictly a war-fighting approach. However, there is also the view that a name change would not be a good idea since the fundamental purpose of the geographic combatant commands is to execute effective joint military combat operations. Strategic messaging would be necessary with any name change to ensure that it does not appear as US disengagement, specifically among our allies and partners. It is also appropriate that the current nomenclature be examined to determine if a name change is sufficiently advantageous.

2. Allies and partners could play a more significant role in geographic combatant commands. Allies and partners should fill positions (including key leadership roles, and exchange and liaison positions) within the geographic combatant command headquarters structure. International involvement could strengthen allied and partner nation support for US policy in the region and improve pre-positioning and posture opportunities. Allies and partners might also be better positioned to support the US message. Australian contributions at Pacific Command (PACOM), for example, can be used as a model for allied and partner nation involvement. Currently, Australians hold just over thirty positions in PACOM, including several key leadership roles.[10] Allied/partner involvement would allow Department of State regional bureaus an additional

9   Government Accountability Office, "Interagency Collaboration: Key Issues for Congressional Oversight of National Security Strategies, Organizations, Workforce, and Information Sharing," http://www.gao.gov/products/GAO-09-904SP.

10 Sheridan Kearnan, Minister Counselor, Defense Policy, Australian Defense Staff, Washington, remarks to Atlantic Council task force, January 16, 2014.

Figure 1. Departments of Defense and State Areas of Responsibility

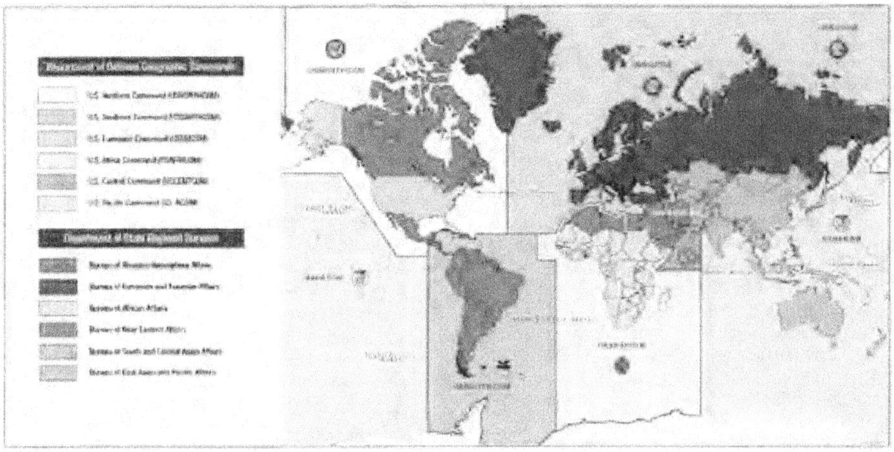

Source: *Joint Force Quarterly.*

means of interface. However, allied and partner involvement should not be limited to integration at geographic combatant commands. They should also be involved with and included in strategic planning with Department of Defense, Department of State, and other agencies and departments. Allies and partners should be involved with strategy reviews and force planning at the highest levels in order to meet the emerging twenty-first-century strategic and fiscal realities.

3. Geographic combatant commanders should be assigned for sufficient time (at least three or four years) to gain a deeper understanding of the region and help fortify relations with regional counterparts. Currently, most commanders serve for two to three years. Relationships with US allies and partners make a difference and longevity enables commands to be effective and efficient at accomplishing core functions. It is also imperative that geographic combatant commanders have regional experience and are allowed sufficient time to prepare before taking command. As the United States progresses toward a more prominent role for regional diplomats, military commanders must also be more steeped in regional matters under their purview.

4. Divergence of regional boundaries among the Department of Defense, Department of State, and National Security Council causes friction and confusion. A common "map" would enhance a whole-of-government approach. Currently, US government agencies and departments must

coordinate with many different organizations in their planning efforts. The number of organizations is increased due to a lack of alignment among regional boundaries within these agencies and departments.

The 2011 National Defense Authorization Act required the comptroller general of the United States to conduct a study to assess the need for and implications of a common alignment of world regions in the internal organization of departments and agencies of the federal government with international responsibilities.[11] The GAO study addressed the advantages and disadvantages of a common geographic alignment as well as obstacles to implementing a common alignment. Geographic alignment is primarily based on the ability to achieve agency-specific mission objectives, to reflect commonalities among countries with cultural, historic, or economic connections, and to address management issues (e.g., balanced workloads) within the organizations.[12] According to the study, all of the agencies indicated that they needed to maintain the flexibility to reorganize geographic alignments to better meet mission requirements. One of the primary advantages of a common geographic alignment would be that there would

11 National Defense Authorization Act 2011, http://www.gpo.gov/fdsys/pkg/PLAW-111publ383/pdf/PLAW-111publ383.pdf.

12 Government Accountability Office, "Interagency Collaboration: Implications of a Common Alignment of World Regions among Select Federal Agencies," http://www.gao.gov/assets/100/97628.pdf.

48

All Elements of National Power

be a decrease in the number of organizations to coordinate with when conducting operations. One of the primary disadvantages of a common alignment would be that it would limit the ability for organizations to realign themselves based on mission objectives.

A common alignment would facilitate a whole-of-government approach and would lay the foundation for effective interagency collaboration. As difficult as this may be to achieve due to cultural practices and concerns in individual agencies, it should be made a priority for the greater good of the nation. A study should be commissioned to determine the most appropriate geographic alignment that would represent the majority of the interagency organizations. This approach would foster an alignment that would not overly emphasize a specific national instrument of power over another.

Efficiencies

1. Certain regionally prepositioned supplies and equipment should be managed in a more coordinated manner by departments and agencies. Integrated prepositioning would save money/manpower, eliminate redundancies, and provide for a synchronized approach to crisis response resulting in quicker reaction times. For example, USAID humanitarian supplies could be colocated with geographic combatant command supplies, as long as there are similar storage requirements. Colocated supplies and equipment would eliminate redundancies and provide for an expeditious and synchronized approach to crisis response resulting in quicker reaction times.

2. There are potentially major efficiencies that can be gained by returning "back office" functions from the geographic combatant commands and their service component commands to the Services and Joint Staff and otherwise streamlining geographic combatant command headquarters staffs. Geographic combatant commands have a fundamental requirement to operate and their organizational structure should focus primarily on operations. Over the past ten years, regional combatant commands have grown significantly due to increasing mission requirements and there is now a strong need to prioritize, restructure, and eliminate redundancies. A GAO study confirmed that authorized military and civilian positions increased by about 50 percent from fiscal

years 2001 through 2012, to about 10,100 authorized positions. In addition, mission and headquarters support costs at the combatant commands more than doubled from fiscal years 2007 through 2012, to about $1.1 billion.[13] Returning "back-office" functions, such as personnel, travel processing, human relations, resource allocation and programming, and communications, to the services and joint staff could facilitate reducing some of these rising costs.

The Department of Defense can also gain efficiencies by eliminating redundancies and duplication of effort between geographic combatant commands and component headquarters. Directorates J2 (Intelligence), J5 (Strategy, Plans & Policy), and J8 (Resources & Assessment) should all be specifically addressed for redundancies between the headquarters staffs. Additionally, the role of combat support agencies, such as the Defense Logistics Agency and Defense Intelligence Agency, should be evaluated in terms of redundancies and duplication of effort in their support to geographic combatant commands. However, it is critical that resources are aligned with mission requirements. Under the current and future fiscal environment, it may be necessary to shed resourcing of less defense-centric roles and activities to ensure there is appropriate focus on the core functions. A geographic combatant command must have the ability to function efficiently and effectively during crisis response as well. A rapidly deployable augmentation capability that is trained and ready to support the geographic combatant commands in times of crisis is critical to this approach.

Finally, the United States needs to evaluate long-term cost savings associated with significant reductions in contract support to the geographic combatant commands. A GAO study recently confirmed that the availability of data on the number of contractor personnel or full-time equivalents varied across the combatant commands, and thus trends could not be identified.[14] Unfortunately, combatant commands have not been required to maintain historical data on the number of contractor personnel. The secretary of defense and chairman of the Joint Chiefs of Staff should charter a qualified outside group to critically assess the status quo and report back in sixty to ninety days.

13 Government Accountability Office, "DOD Needs to Periodically Review and Improve Visibility of Combatant Commands' Resources," http://www.gao.gov/assets/660/654638.pdf.
14 Ibid.

SPECIFIC RESTRUCTURING OPTIONS

The task force also evaluated three specific restructuring options that would help move US regional presence toward a more effective interagency balance. With any structure changes, strategic messaging as well as education and training would be required for all personnel. Although these restructuring options require legislative and behavioral change and are a move away from long-standing institutional norms, they are worthy of discussion and should be evaluated based on emerging twenty-first-century strategic and fiscal realities.

Unconventional end-state: interagency regional center

The unconventional approach highlights the issues that the United States should be thinking about to fully move toward a regional interagency balance. If the United States were to start over and completely redefine how it approached foreign and defense policy execution and the advancement of US interests at the regional level, what would it look like? Although this may be the most difficult option to execute in the near to medium term, it is useful to analyze and assess a regional structure if the United States wiped the slate clean. This bold option will take time and effort to build interagency stakeholder buy-in and may be difficult for agencies to adapt.

An unconventional end-state would be the creation of an "Interagency Regional Center" (IRC) that would act as a regional interagency headquarters for foreign and defense policy. This new organization would result in the unification of the Department of Defense and the Department of State (as well as other agencies and departments) at the regional level (see figure 2). The IRC would be led by an "interagency regional director" with deep regional experience and expertise who would report directly to the president or vice president of the United States. The president develops the grand strategy and establishes national security strategy, while the regional directors would implement that strategy at the regional level. The regional directors would advise and participate in the National Security Council as requested. Regional directors would also convene to discuss cross-regional issues and activities as required. The IRCs would ensure long-lasting integration of all instruments of national power.

An IRC would ideally be forward-located within the region and would provide implementation support for country ambassadors and country teams. The IRC would be responsible for orchestrating and enforcing presidential policy and guidance. Departments and agencies outside of the IRC would still have the responsibility to organize, train, equip, acquire, and maintain capabilities as well as formulate policies to support presidential guidance. The interagency regional directors (IRDs) would retain overall authority and responsibility for execution of regional foreign and defense policy.

Figure 2. Unconventional End-State: Interagency Regional Center

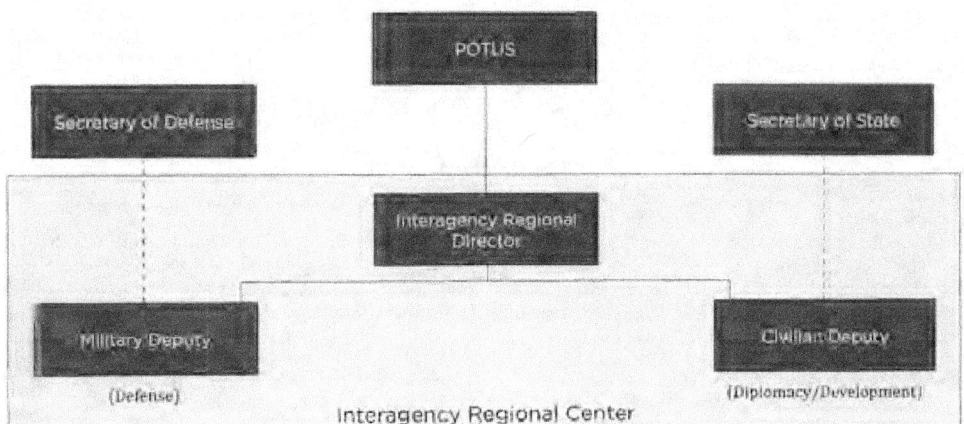

All Elements of National Power

Figure 3. Intermediate Approach: Colocation

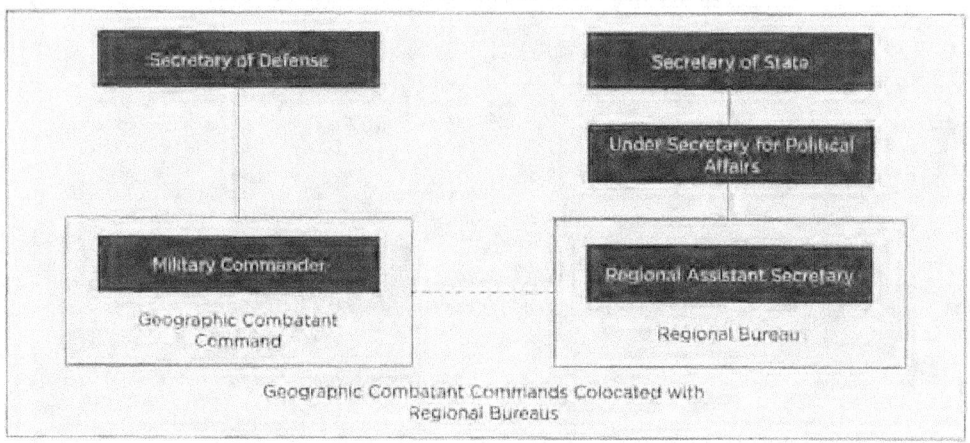

The IRD would have a military and civilian deputy. The military deputy would focus on defense issues while the civilian deputy would focus on diplomacy, development, and other critical nonmilitary issues. The civilian deputy would also act as a regional ambassador-at-large who would have coordination authority for country ambassadors and other civilian-led departments such as Treasury, Justice, and Commerce. Country ambassadors would still formally report directly to the secretary of state through the IRC. The civilian deputy would be in charge of coordinating all nonmilitary agency activity at the regional level. During wartime, the military commander would report directly to the president through the secretary of defense as in the current combatant command structure, while the director and civilian deputy would focus on institution-building and post-conflict operations. During peacetime, the military would report to the secretary of defense through the IRC for peacetime engagement. For this approach to be successful, peacetime and wartime responsibilities would need to be clearly delineated and understood.

A unified organization would improve both defense and diplomatic planning processes and coordination on the use of scarce resources. The IRC would integrate and synchronize both Department of Defense and Department of State objectives within the region. This structure should also assist in accommodating funding differences between the Department of Defense and the Department of State. Currently, unequal resourcing between the Department of Defense and the Department of State creates significant roadblocks to enhancing interagency presence at the regional level. Under the new structure, the "Interagency Integrated Priority List" would better balance defense, diplomacy, and development issues.

Intermediate approach: Colocate geographic combatant commands and regional bureaus

Another option is an intermediate approach that would promote greater unity of effort without creating a new organization. This approach would colocate the Department of State regional bureaus with the geographic combatant commands (see figure 3). Currently, all Department of State regional bureaus are located in Washington, DC. This intermediate approach would move the regional assistant secretary and his/her staff to the same location as the geographic combatant commands, strengthen the authority of regional bureaus, and allow the bureaus to operate more nimbly.

An alternative would be to move a deputy regional assistant secretary and staff to the geographic combatant command, and leave the regional assistant secretary and some staff in Washington, DC. This deputy assistant secretary would have direct contact with the regional assistant secretary, but would be forward-based with the geographic combatant command. Although not ideal, due to the significant difference in rank structure between the military commander (four-star) and a deputy assistant secretary, this alternative option may be more palatable to some Department of State officials.

Colocation of other departments and agencies, such as CIA regional offices, should also be considered. Colocation would allow for integration of the Department of Defense and the Department of State (as well as other key agencies and departments) at the regional level. Countries in the region would enjoy a more unified approach and presence among US government departments and agencies.

Figure 4. Intermediate Approach: Coordination Authority

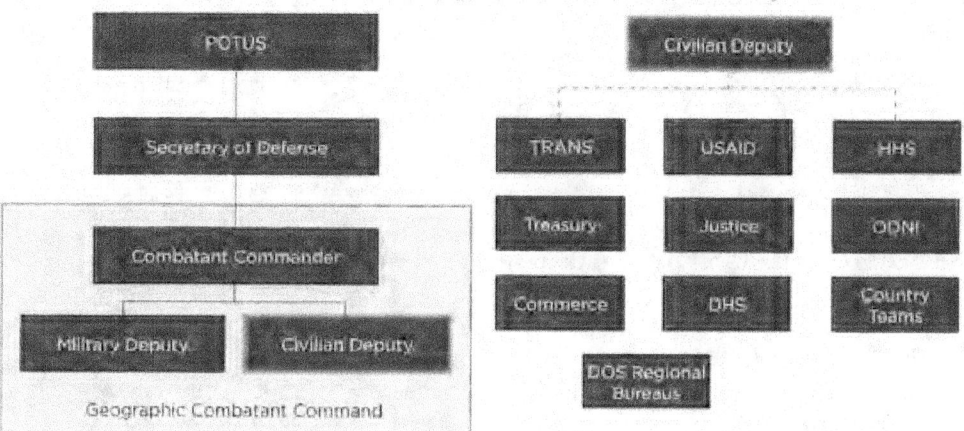

Possible limitations to this approach would be that some international partners would see the move as a "militarization of US foreign policy" and the regional assistant secretaries becoming subordinate to the military. Because of the difference in the number of military personnel versus civilian diplomatic personnel working at the center, the image presented to visiting diplomats may be that they are visiting a military headquarters versus a diplomatic regional center. Strategic messaging would be critical to ensuring the success of this approach. While colocation may provide more integration at the regional level, it may still lack the overall strategic coordination and integration of policies in Washington. Additionally, a common map between the Department of Defense and the Department of State would be required to facilitate this approach.

Intermediate approach: Civilian deputy with coordination authority

An alternative intermediate approach would be for the geographic combatant command civilian deputy to act as a regional ambassador-at-large that would have coordination authority for country ambassadors and other civilian-led organizations (see figure 4) in the region. This approach builds a civilian perspective into the combatant commands and establishes a stronger civilian voice into the combatant command structure.

The civilian deputy's mandate under this authority would be to coordinate US actions, issues, and initiatives within the region and bordering regions. The civilian deputy would coordinate all executive department and agency activity within the region in the development and implementation of US foreign and defense policies. The civilian deputy would have the authority to require consultation between regional organizations but would

not have the authority to compel agreement. This authority would be a coordinating relationship, not an authority through which chain of command would be exercised. This approach works under the current structure but adds integration by bringing together all agencies operating within the region to coordinate regional activities. A strong relationship between the civilian deputy and the regional assistant secretary would be essential for the success of this approach.

CONCLUSION

Long-range global trends and near-term security challenges demand a more sophisticated use of the instruments of national power. The United States needs to move toward a regional interagency balance for engaging with key allies and partners that improves efficiency and effectiveness of US foreign and defense policy execution and advance US interests at the regional level. It is critical that the United States think about how to adapt to emerging twenty-first-century realities, both strategic and fiscal, particularly as it transitions from a decade at war. The United States must better take advantage of its strategic assets, and resource and restructure for a more balanced, forward-deployed regional approach.

Although the recommendations and options presented in this report are not necessarily the whole solution—nor will they be easy to implement—it is necessary to open the discussion about better aligning our national interagency structure to be ready for the next set of asymmetrical challenges. The members of the task force hope that this report will help stimulate a serious discussion inside and outside of government.

The secretary of defense, chairman of the Joint Chiefs of Staff, the secretary of state, and the national security advisor should commission a follow-on study to further evaluate and make actionable the key insights and recommendations of this report.

53

coordination. I believe that a look at the National Security Council and how it is

Mr. JONES. Thank you, sir.
The last point, the whole-of-government

resourced and what it does must be included in any Goldwater-Nichols review. New global challenges require interagency response not former stovepipe solutions. For example, early in 2009, we combined the Department of Homeland Security staff with the National Security staff in recognition of the fact that security threats are not contained by borders. But the new National Security staff was awarded an anemic budget of $4 million to perform the task at hand, which is was absolutely impossible. We were able to get a modest increase, but a detailed study in 2010 suggested that $23 million would be appropriate to create a small NSC [National Security Council] staff with agency-like functions and expertise to do the job.

But the overwhelming difficulty with the NSC is one of management of personnel, not so much the size, although I recognize that it needs to be reformed. The detailees who are assigned to the NSC are there for very short periods of time, and in 2010, because of the lack of funding to pay salaries and compensation for the entire staff, most of the people at the NSC were detailees from other agencies and they were allowed to stay for about a year. So in 2010, 50 percent of the National Security Council rotated back to their parent agencies and was replaced. My view is that three-quarters of the people in the NSC ought to be permanent personnel, and one-fourth ought to be augmentees from the agencies. Today it is exactly the opposite.

I believe that the National Security Council must be a policy communicating, disseminating organization, not one that micromanages implementation, and we should avoid that micromanagement. But it is a slippery slope that all NSCs eventually have to confront as they mature in any administration. It must serve as a coordinating agency to effectuate the national security policies that require presidential decisions.

Secretary Gates in his testimony underscored the important role of the NSC and the National Security staff as a presidential instrument ensuring proper implementation by the interagency. Destructive consequences of DOD and national security interests pertaining to partisan gridlock, budget impasses, and the recurring threat of government shutdowns was also emphasized.

Mr. Chairman, Senator Reed, thank you very much for inviting me to be here today. I firmly believe that your work is an important work. It will serve the country well for the next 30 years, and I would recommend use of the original Goldwater-Nichols architects in the Defense Reform Task Force to make a major contribution to a new Goldwater-Nichols, as all are still current on the issues and all are still very influential and providing wise advice to our government.

Thank you.

[The prepared statement of Mr. Jones follows:]

PREPARED STATEMENT BY GENERAL JAMES L. JONES, USMC (RET)

Chairman McCain, Senator Reed, Members of the Committee, thank you for inviting me to add to the expert testimony you have already received from the staff architects of one of the most significant pieces of legislation affecting America's Armed Forces and their civilian leadership: The Goldwater–Nichols Department of Defense Reorganization Act (GNA) of 1986.

As you know, the GNA's purpose was to modernize the Department of Defense to fulfill its national security roles and missions in changing times. Modernization, of course, is an enduring obligation. It requires an iterative and ongoing process of examination—one that responds with agility to national experience and lessons learned, yielding reforms that meet the unique circumstances and requirements of our time.

So, I commend the Committee for its leadership in undertaking this analysis of what changes are necessary based on today's new and swiftly evolving security needs. I hope that some observations from my experience in and out of uniform will be of service to you in this task.

From 1979–1984, I was privileged to serve as the Marine Corps Senate Liaison Officer, under the leadership of then-Captain John McCain who directed the combined Navy-Marine Corps Liaison Office until he retired from active duty in 1980. In many ways, my time on Capitol Hill was among the most educational experiences of my 40-year active-duty career that culminated in my serving as Commandant of the Marine Corps (Service Chief function), Commander of the U.S. European Command (Combatant Commander function), and in NATO as Supreme Allied Commander, Europe (Command of NATO's 26 nation, multinational force). After I retired from active duty in 2007, I served as Special Envoy for Middle East Regional Security until 2008. From 2009 -2010, I was privileged to serve as National Security Advisor.

The first days of my Capitol Hill assignment coincided with the advent of GNA, the early days of the creation of the All-Volunteer Force (AVF), and the transition to joint force concepts. Over the next five years, I had the good fortune of working with and knowing many Members of Congress and their staff, as well as the principal architects of the GNA legislation, some of whom have already testified on the subject at hand. Many of these relationships blossomed into lifelong friendships that I continue to treasure to this day.

With regard to my appearance before the committee today, I wish to identify myself with the testimony offered by Mr. James R Locher lll, Major General Arnold L Punaro USMCR (Ret), and Dr. John J Hamre. Likewise, Secretary Michael Donley, here today, was among those who, throughout his distinguished career, contributed significantly to the passage and implementation of Goldwater-Nichols. Though many Members and staff participated in the development of Goldwater-Nichols, the contribution and expertise of these former members of the SASC Staff to this legislation is beyond question. Each of them continues to offer wise counsel to current leadership of the Department of Defense today.

I agree fully with the testimony of these experts. It is not my intent to repeat the content of their valuable contribution, phrased in different words. Rather, I would hope to be helpful to the Committee
in making a few points gathered from the experience of serving in the senior military positions I previously mentioned.

TIME FOR REFORM

The Goldwater-Nichols Act reformed a Department of Defense that operated for nearly 40 years under the mandate of the National Security Act of 1947. In the nearly 30 years that have elapsed since GNA's passage, America's Armed Forces have been asked to do much in a world that has changed significantly, and with it the national security threats we face and requirements to combat them.

Until this Committee's current efforts, the most comprehensive review of GNA and its ''unintended consequences'' across the Department was commissioned in 1997 by then-Secretary of Defense William Cohen, when I served as his Senior Military Assistant.

MajGen Punaro's testimony earlier this month recounts the team that was assembled—the Defense Reform Task Force—and its work at Secretary Cohen's behest. While 18 years old that study still stands, in my opinion, as the best effort to date in identifying Goldwater-Nichols impacts and reforms. I highly recommend that this Committee revisit the Task Force's findings as you undertake the task of modernizing the Department and our military forces to face 21st century challenges.

In the course of this work we should remember very distinctly that the Senate passed the GNA by a vote of 95–0. This overwhelming consensus was achieved despite strong objections from Department of Defense civilian and military leadership of the time. This clearly suggests that any future revision of Goldwater-Nichols should again be undertaken objectively and externally to the Department of Defense for several reasons.

First, the Department is consumed with everyday problems around the globe; they are mounting in complexity and frequency, suggesting that there isn't enough time for a study of this magnitude to be accomplished ''inside'' the Pentagon. However, the Pentagon should very much be invited to participate fully and in complete transparency in any notional ''Goldwater-Nichols ll'' effort. Second, large bureaucracies have inherent difficulty in implementing ''change'' from within. Our senior leaders rotate out of their positions frequently, leaving behind the entrenched middle-level management which, normally, will always attempt to hold the line against truly significant reform. Third, some of the necessary remaining reforms pertaining to the original legislation will challenge entrenched interests who will fiercely resist many of the recommendations proposed by previous witnesses, including my own.

FOUR CRITICAL FOCUS AREAS IN NEED OF URGENT EXAMINAION

In order to not duplicate the previous testimonies with which I largely agree, I would like to focus my input on four areas requiring urgent examination and consideration for reform in any effort to produce "Goldwater-Nichols ll" legislation aimed at improving the ability to provide for the nation's security.

One, the overwhelming and unsustainable "all in" personnel costs associated with the All-Volunteer Force and the dangers that systemic imbalances pose to the Department's capacities and capabilities.

Two, the wasteful and inefficient manner that the Department of Defense conducts its "business," requiring that we reevaluate the utility of the Defense Department's own agencies as currently tasked and organized.

Three, the compelling need to move toward a new interagency balance centered around reformed "Unified Commands," now titled Combatant Commands.

Four, the requirement to modernize the role, mission, and organization of the National Security Council (NSC). Though not specifically addressed in the Goldwater-Nichols Act of 1986, the critical role played by the NSC in the formulation of national security policy should be considered as a necessary part of any "Goldwater-Nichols ll" effort.

1) Unsustainable "All In" Personnel Costs Threaten the Efficacy of the All–Volunteer Force

The past three Secretaries of Defense (Gates, Panetta, and Hagel), have each publicly stated that the cost growth of personnel expenditures, in general, is unsustainable. As noted in MajGen Punaro's testimony, their conclusions are based on the "comparison of the 1998 to 2014 cost growth in military pay, quality of life, retired pay, and VA and DOD health care which far exceeded both the GDP and the Employment Cost Index."

The problem in my view is more serious than commonly recognized. I would submit that the results of the Military Compensation and Retirement Modernization Commission's Interim Report have been, in part, overlooked as it pertains to the actual cost of programs. These costs are reflected in a well-documented chart showing that "the actual costs for pay, benefits, health care, and retirement, was over $400 billion a year, and that there is a $1 trillion unfunded liability over the next ten years in a military retirement fund that is not in any budget." Given the current fiscal strains in a time requiring greater national security resources, these are sobering facts.

By way of example, when I served as Commandant of the Marine Corps from 1999–2003, I recall that almost 50 percent of the Marine Corps' annual budget was consumed by the aforementioned "personnel costs." At the time I worried about the long-term trend of such costs as it was evident that they were destined to climb rapidly, most likely at the expense of the core competency of the Marine Corps' most urgent mission, that of producing an unrivaled fighting force to meet the future needs of the nation. Today, our current Commandant, General Robert B. Neller, is challenged by the reality of having to spend 68 percent of his budget on those same costs. This means that in the 13 years since I left that office "all in" personnel costs have increased by approximately 18 percent. It also means that Gen Neller has 18 percent less resources to spend on the requisite training and equipping of today's Marine Corps. If left unchecked, this disturbing trend will accelerate, weakening the Marine Corps' capabilities to fulfill its roles and missions.

Dr. Hamre, MajGen Punaro, and Mr. Locher have provided accurate and valuable insights into the situation and the catastrophic consequences of failing to address the calamitous growth in personnel costs. Fortunately, there are several remedies which warrant serious examination. Among these are the need to modernize the pay and benefits for the active duty, reserve, DOD civilian, and retired communities. Serious work has already been done towards better understanding the urgency of the current situation.

The body of evidence strongly points to the folly of superimposing the All-Volunteer Force on what was essentially a conscripted system. In retrospect this was probably short-sighted given that today we are harnessed with a raft of requirements developed for a different kind of force in a bygone era, including guaranteeing equal pay regardless of quality of work, a retirement system based only on 20 and 30 years of service, and a health care system that benefitted personnel serving on active duty, and those having achieved "retired eligibility" status. The eligibility qualifications in all three areas have been enhanced, but remain essentially unchanged despite the increase in the numbers of eligible recipients who are also living much longer than the GNA ever anticipated.

FUNDING DOD'S "TAIL" AT THE EXPENSE OF THE "TOOTH"

While I do not want to belabor points this committee has heard in previous testimony, the monumental impact of the Department's ballooning all-in costs of personnel can't be overstated. The problem stands as among the greatest threats to the Department's ability to maintain a balanced "tooth-to-tail" ratio between the war fighting forces and the support establishment. The status quo threatens the Department's ability to maintain U.S. national security and it demands urgent attention.

The significant increase of the Department's headquarters' staff—"the tail"—including civilians, military, and contractors has created a stifling bureaucracy, yielded processes and procedures that are far too complex to perform once simple tasks. The dynamic has produced a paralyzing environment in which micro-management and endless consensus building impede initiative and impede action. Moreover the "tail" is soaking up resources needed by the "teeth" of our armed forces.

Resources once allocated to recruiting, training, and equipping front line forces are now being reallocated to support the increasingly top-heavy headquarters' components. When considering total personnel in the support establishment associated with the Office of the Secretary of Defense, the Joint Staff, the Combatant Commands and the Defense Agencies, the Department of Defense spends $113 billion to support 240,000 people. Referencing once again MajGen Punaro's previous testimony to further illustrate my point, in 1958, the size of the Joint Staff was authorized for and limited to 400 personnel. Today, we support upwards of 4,000 across the J-directorates. At the height of the military build-up under President Ronald Reagan, $600 billion was spent in support of 2.2 million active duty service members. Today, in constant dollars, $600 billion supports only 1.2 million troops.

Funding the military health care system is one of the Department of Defense's largest annual expenditures. When we consider the fact that medical treatment facilities are operating only at 50 percent utilization rate, but have on staff a division's worth of medical administrators, one has to question the justification of more than $41.7 billion budget allocated each year to the Defense Health Program.

Addressing the inequities in our military compensation and benefits system is now necessary and overdue, and I note that some much needed efforts are already underway to address this important issue. Consideration should be given to the relationship between active duty pay and entitlements and any earned retirement benefits that are representative of a more modern system.

It is important to be very clear about one fact: I feel very strongly that, in fairness, all who serve today on active or reserve duty should remain eligible for retirement benefits under the terms currently in force. Studies have shown that even with this stipulation, billions of dollars could be saved by implementing a new program for all future service members who enter the Armed Services "tomorrow."

Across the Department of Defense, we are spending far more resources on the "tail" and far too little on the "tooth". In any event, the spiraling "ALL IN" personnel costs need to be considered as a single entity, and not as unrelated stovepipes, which has been the tradition for the past several decades.

MANDATE ACQUISITION REFORM

Acquisition reform is another area which is in need of urgent reform. While there are many ways to address this issue, starting with the costs and the length of time it takes to produce the next generation of ground, sea, and air weapons systems, culminating with the layered bureaucracy that manages the business end of procurement in the Pentagon, simple logic and observation suggests that our acquisition process as a whole is either dysfunctional, broken, or both. One need only to look at the Air Force F–35 program, the Marine Corps' ill-fated AAAV program, the Navy's Ford Class Carrier program, and the Army's Future Combat Systems program to recognize that there is unsustainable enormous waste and inefficiency in the costs and length of time it takes to travel the road from concept to operational delivery of many of our major programs. This process can and must be fixed.

As a former service chief, I can tell the Committee first hand that my inability to influence the acquisition of major war-fighting end items was easily the most frustrating aspect of my tenure as Commandant. In fact, even though I was prohibited from any participation in the acquisition process by congressional fiat, I was nonetheless summoned on several occasions to testify about the costs, progress, and difficulties within our major programs, an acquisition responsibility I did not have at the time.

This committee has already taken a necessary step forward in this year's National Defense Authorization Act by reinstating Service Chiefs into the acquisition process and by placing upon them the complete responsibility for their service programs. As Dr. Hamre highlighted in his testimony recently, "DOD often courts trouble when there are confused or bifurcated responsibilities for functions and activities. It made no sense to have the Service Chiefs responsible for training, equipping and housing their respective forces, but not be accountable for acquisition.''

2) THE PENTAGON'S BUSINESS PRACTICES ARE ANTIQUATED

Several of our Defense Support Agencies, perhaps created to satisfy relevant needs of the time, have outlived their usefulness. At almost every turn, we have avoided the serious reforms that are urgently needed and could, if enacted, produce huge savings. ''Today, DOD Agencies' expenditures are in excess of 20 percent of the entire defense budget'', according to MajGen Punaro's testimony, ''and have a cumulative headcount of over 400,000 active duty military, defense civilians, and contractors.''

My most defining experience with such defense support agencies occurred in 2002, specifically with the Defense Logistics Agency (DLA), when the Marine Corps became the first service since the Vietnam War to modernize the field uniform, which had become too expensive to produce and maintain.

After significant research, we found that new textile products would allow us to produce a new field uniform that was both cheaper for the Marine Corps and less costly for Marines to maintain. Initially, in accordance with the Department's standard operating procedure, I approached DLA for support. Upon asking DLA for a cost estimate for production of a new uniform, we discovered that DLA's ''carrying charge'' for this service would be 22%. This was the ''surcharge'' to each service for the ''privilege'' of doing our business for us. A simple check of ''industry wide standards'' for similar middle-man services revealed that the costs should have been approximately 6%. I made the decision to produce the new uniform within the Marine Corps itself, with a very small group of Marines, which we did, and at a significantly lower cost to the Service itself than the old uniform, and at a substantial savings in maintenance cost for all Marines.

A second memorable experience from my time as Service Chief relates to the role and functions of the Department of Defense's own agencies, many of which have long since outlived their usefulness and currently contribute little to the war-fighting capabilities of our Armed Forces. Consider, as MajGen Punaro testified, that ''Defense Agencies are Big Business''. Five of the Department of Defense's top ten clients are its own agencies, and its top two clients are the DLA and the Defense Health Programs (DHP). Lockheed Martin Corporation occupies the third spot on DOD's top ten clients.

Defense Agencies are Big Business		
Rank	Defense Agency/Defense Contractor	Agency Budget/Contract Awards ($B)
1	Defense Logistics Agency (DLA)	$44.1
2	Defense Health Program (DHP)	$41.7
3	Lockheed Martin Corporation	$28.2
4	Boeing Corporation	$22.5
5	Northrop Grumman	$14.2
6	General Dynamics Corporation	$10.6
7	Raytheon	$10.2
8	Defense Information Systems Agency (DISA)	$9.4
9	Missile Defense Agency (MDA)	$7.6
10	Defense Commissary Agency (DeCA)	$7.3
11	United Technologies Corporation	$5.7
12	Halliburton	$5.4
13	Stewart & Stevenson	$5.1
14	L-3 Communications	$3.8
15	SAIC	$3.6
16	General Electric	$3.6
17	BAE Systems	$3.5
18	Humana	$3.0
19	Defense Advanced Research Project Agency (DARPA)	$2.9
20	Defense Education Activity (DODEA)	$2.6

*Contractor data is prime contracts with DOD from federal contract database.

MajGen Punaro goes on to inform us that the ''DLA does over $44 billion a year of business with DOD while Lockheed Martin is a distant third at $28 billion.''

He further states that ''most of the Department's defense agencies would rate in the Fortune 250 and several are in the Fortune 50. They are not managed as businesses ... even though one is, in fact, a grocery business. Another is a worldwide communications provider, and another on is the world's largest and most expensive health care system (DHP).''

FLAG AND GENERAL OFFICERS SHOULD COMMAND TROOPS, NOT RUN ''BUSINESSES''

A question worth asking is this: Why is it that our largest and most business intensive defense agencies are headed by active duty flag and general officers? It would seem that leadership, direction, and fiscal solvency of such agencies would be greatly enhanced by having in the agencies' most senior positions leaders who actually have the experience of successfully managing large businesses. They would benefit significantly by the accountability and continuity of stable leadership than the current difficulties associated with transient military personnel who move in and out of such leadership assignments very rapidly. Excess military personnel derived from such reforms would be identified and returned to the operational ranks of their respective service, further enhancing the ''tooth-to-tail'' ratio.

Overall, however, we should ask the hard questions as to why several agencies remain operational at all. For example, the 10th largest client of DOD, the Defense Commissary Agency (DCA) operates as a subsidized entity at a cost to the taxpayer of $1.4 billion, annually. Why would we not ''outsource'' our military on-base ''grocery stores'' to a major grocery chain that could run the operation without a subsidy, at reduced cost, and with more savings for military families. As Commandant of the Marine Corps, I volunteered my service to experiment with the concept of outsourcing our commissaries in 2001. However, the offer was not accepted, largely because of entrenched interests opposed to this idea, coupled with limited time I had remaining as a Service Chief in early 2003.

How the Department of Defense does its business is very much worthy of review in any effort to construct a meaningful revision to GNA.

3) REBALANCING THE INTERAGENCY AND THE UNIFIED COMMANDS TO MEET 21ST CENTURY THREATS

Dr. Hamre's testimony identified some interesting ideas concerning the Combatant Commands and their evolution since GNA was adopted. I would like submit for consideration several suggestions on transforming our Unified Commands to better reflect the realities of their missions and the deployment of national assets to enhance the global engagement effectiveness of the United States in the 21st century.

From 2003–2007, I was privileged to serve as NATO's Supreme Allied Commander (SACEUR) and as Commander United States European Command (EUCOM). All totaled, this responsibility included in excess of 80 countries. What is not as well known is that this assignment also included the entire African continent, but excluded the countries comprising the Horn of Africa. Interestingly, at the time of my command, the word ''Africa'' did not appear in the title ''U.S. European Command''. The Deputy Commander of this command, for most of my tenure, was Gen. Charles Wald, USAF. His leadership and commitment to our entire geographical area of responsibility, including Africa, was critical to the transformation of the command in supporting the war-fighting efforts in Afghanistan and Iraq, as well as the eventual creation of the U.S. Africa Command (AFRICOM). Gen. Wald's insistence that the African continent's emergence on the world stage as an enormous reality that the United States could no longer ignore was the catalyst to an American awakening to this reality. Future administrations will have to recognize this as one of the most urgent geo-strategic imperatives of the future. Africa has ''arrived,'' and its potential is enormous; this should be good news for the United States, as well as an increasingly urgent challenge.

The idea for AFRICOM, which was devised by EUCOM, was based on a simple premise. Gen Wald and I concluded that EUCOM's mission at the time was too vast, especially if we were to devote the required attention to the growing terrorist threats that were surfacing in different regions in Africa. We proposed to Secretary Donald Rumsfeld the idea for creating AFRICOM. Coupled with this idea was the recommendation that if created, AFRICOM should be located on the African continent. We also recommended that we should not call it a ''Combatant Command,'' as this title alone would make it more difficult to find a ''home'' in Africa. We proposed referring to it by what I strongly feel is the correct title for all such geographical commands: a Unified Command. Today, AFRICOM has a home in Stuttgart, Germany alongside EUCOM. This is not ideal from a geographically strategic standpoint. All geographical commands are still referred to a ''Combatant Commands,'' inaccurately in my view. With your permission I will hereinafter refer to such commands as ''Unified Commands.''

The presence of our six geographical Unified Commands on several different continents is a gift of the 20th century, a privilege no other country in the world enjoys. The Unified Command structure emerged after the end of World War ll, when confidence in the United States as a country to be admired and associated with was at its zenith. For its values, its refusal to permanently occupy defeated adversaries, and democratic principles that celebrated the potential of each individual fortunate to be called "American," America became the global model for the future.

Today, our Unified Commands remain uniquely valuable assets that continue to foster military interoperability and training, common military architectures, and requisite support to our friends and allies. For these commands to be able to achieve their maximum potential effectiveness, I believe they should be geographically located in the regions they hope to affect.

In the past years, we have witnessed the transition of the United States Southern Command (SOUTHCOM) from Panama to Florida, and the United States Central Command (CENTCOM) operating only a forward headquarters element in Qatar with the predominance of its forces operating in Tampa, Florida. Today, only USEUCOM (Stuttgart, Germany), and the United States Pacific Command (Hawaii) are the two unified commands that can claim to be located in the geographical regions of their responsibility. I recognize the inherent difficulty in reversing decisions already taken, but I would highly recommend that, if possible, CENTCOM and AFRICOM find homes in their respective regions of responsibility as a matter of urgency.

In the Middle East, the influence and reputation of the United States has suffered in the eyes of our friends and allies in the region. Generally speaking, it is the widespread view that the Unites States has rebalanced its priorities to the Pacific at the expense of what many feel is the most dangerous region on Earth, the Middle East. It is true that the home of the United States Navy's Fifth Fleet is still Bahrain, and that CENTCOM still maintains a forward headquarters in Qatar. We have smaller task forces sprinkled in several countries in the region, but the absence of CENTCOM itself in the region has created a vacuum. This calls into question our national resolve to play a constructive role in a crisis-torn part of the world with enormous security challenges now and in the future.

The regional decline in confidence in the United States has opened up the previously unthinkable possibility that our historical friends and allies are actually seeking assistance from, and closer relations with, Russia, China, and several European countries. In Africa, we surrendered in 1990 the top trading position we used to enjoy to China. Today, the oft-repeated refrain from many African leaders to their American counterparts is "Where are you? Why aren't you in my country? We need America in Africa!"

Much has been done in the preceding two administrations towards reversing this negative trend, but much more needs to be done. I am not just speaking about United States military presence or stepping up the activities of our foreign and civil services in Africa, but the presence of our companies, NGOs, and academic institutions. As part of this overall effort, successfully placing AFRICOM in Africa would send a very powerful message to the continent's 54 countries, that we are "present for duty" as a whole-of-government; and that we intend to be an enduring partner for all African nations seeking freedom and prosperity—objectives which we know depend on the mutually reinforcing pillars of security, economic development, and good governance/rule of law. I would also like to submit for the record a paper I wrote for under the auspices of the Atlantic Council on the need to modernize U.S. global engagement based on these three pillars: security, whole –of-government enterprise, and greater public-private sector cooperation.

Moreover, in July 2014, I chaired as study conducted by the Atlantic Council's Brent Scowcroft Center on International Security entitled "All Elements of National Power; Moving Toward a New Interagency Balance for U.S. Global Engagement." I commend it to this Committee's review. What follows is the executive summary of this study, which suggests that a transformation of our Unified Commands is worthy of consideration in any review of GNA. I request that the full report of the Atlantic Council's study be included as part of my testimony. Copies of the study have been made available to Members and staff of this Committee.

[Questions for the record with answers supplied follow:]

"All Elements of Power; Moving Toward a New Interagency Balance for U.S. Global Engagement" Executive Summary

To deal effectively with long-range global trends and near term securities challenges, the United States requires a broader application of all elements of national power or risks continued disjointed efforts in U.S. global engagement. A transformed interagency balance is a hedge against uncertainty in a dramatically changing world.

As the U.S. National Intelligence Council suggested in its landmark 2012 report, *Global Trends 2030: Alternative Worlds,* tectonic shifts in several theaters will have significant potential to cause global and regional insecurity in the coming decades. American overseas presence in key regions is and will remain integral to meeting the dynamic regional security challenges and specific military threats. The United States faces increased risks and missed opportunities to advance U.S. interests, however, if it continues to focus on the military as the primary government instrument working with allies and partners on a regional scale. The U.S. government currently has only one structure, the geographic combatant command, to execute foreign and defense policy in key regions of the world. At present, there is no mechanism in place to integrate activities of all U.S. government departments and agencies in key regions.

As a result, U.S. gov't regional actions often are uncoordinated and disconnected. To this end, recent geographic combatant commanders have recognized the need for greater interagency coordination and experimented with strengthening the role and relevance of the interagency within their commands. The intent of this report is to go further and make interagency components the key integrator of elements of national power to better manage foreign and defense policy execution. This report discusses how the United States can resource and restructure for a more balanced, forward-deployed regional approach essential in improving the integration of national Instruments of power—diplomatic, informational, military, economic, and others— to advance U.S. interests at the regional level. This task force initially focused solely on restructuring the geographic combatant commands, but it quickly became apparent that higher-priority, untapped points of leverage existed that, if properly resourced, could greatly strengthen U.S. efforts at the regional level. Although these general recommendations are Department of Defense- and Department of State-centric, we recognize the importance for all of us government agencies and departments to play a role in a true "whole-of-government" approach. Initial discussion focuses primarily on security issues with the goal of bringing in the full range of economic, political, and other issues and agencies as changes progress. Many of the recommendations could be implemented in the near- to mid-term under the current structures of the Department of State and the Department of Defense. The following general recommendations were developed toward that end:

Interagency synchronization

- The United States should rebalance national Instruments of power by providing enhanced Department of State capacity in key regions. Unbalanced resourcing and manpower between the Department of Defense and the Department of State creates significant roadblocks to enhancing interagency presence in the region. A more balanced approach would strengthen U.S. engagement more broadly.

- Department of State regional assistant secretaries should be further empowered to set and coordinate foreign policy within the regions. Currently, assistant secretaries have an explicit requirement to be responsible, but they lack sufficient resources and authority to be effective. Regional assistant secretaries should have the authority to integrate the full range of foreign and security policy as well as diplomatic resources to execute foreign policy on a regional scale.

- There should be an ambassador-level civilian deputy in each geographic combatant command with deep regional experience and expertise. Absent crisis or war, the civilian deputy would, on behalf of the commander, oversee and integrate security cooperation efforts with allies and partners. The civilian deputy could also act as the senior political adviser (POLAD) who would have direct liaison with the Department of State regional assistant secretary. Likewise, the senior political-military advisers in the Department of State regional bureaus should have direct "reach-forward" access to applicable geographic combatant command leadership as well as a direct link to civilian deputies/senior POLADs in the geographic combatant commands. If the civilian deputy and senior POLAD are two different positions (depending on combatant command structure), then the civilian deputy would serve as the senior-most civilian representative within the combatant command and the primary link to the Department of State. The senior POLAD would act as the policy adviser to the combatant commander.

- To reach the fullest potential and ensure sustained, effective change, interagency legislation to support these changes would be essential, entailing provisions that would direct departments and agencies to adopt a whole-of-government approach. Legislation could use the Goldwater-Nichols Department of Defense Reorganization Act of 1986 as a model.

Organizational transformation

- Geographic combatant commands should be renamed to signify the importance of a whole-of-government approach. A name change to "unified regional commands" would reinforce efforts to coordinate and integrate instruments of foreign and defense policy execution and would represent broader capabilities and engagement efforts than strictly a war-fighting approach.

- Allies and partners could play a more significant role in geographic combatant commands; international involvement could strengthen allied/partner nation support for U.S. policies and improve prepositioning and posture opportunities.

- Geographic combatant commanders should be assigned for sufficient time (at least three or four years versus two or three years at present) to gain a deeper understanding of the region and help fortify relations with regional counterparts.

- Divergence of regional boundaries among the Department of Defense, Department of State, and National Security Council causes friction and confusion; a common "map" would enhance a whole-of-government approach.

Efficiencies

- Certain regional prepositioned supplies and equipment should be managed in a more coordinated manner by departments and agencies. Integrated prepositioning would save money and manpower, eliminate redundancies, and provide for a synchronized approach to crisis response resulting in quicker reaction times.

- Major efficiencies can be gained by returning "back office" functions from the geographic combatant commands and their service component commands to the Services and the Joint Staff, thereby streamlining geographic combatant command headquarters' staffs. The Secretary of Defense and Chairman of the Joint Chiefs of Staff should request a qualified outside group to assess details in report back in 60 to 90 days.

The task force also evaluated three specific restructuring options that would help move U.S. regional presence toward a more effective interagency balance. Although these restructuring options require legislative and organizational changes and a move away from long-standing institutional norms, they are worthy of discussion and should be evaluated based on emerging 21st century strategic and fiscal realities. The following restructuring options should be explored:

1. An unconventional end-state would be the creation of an "Interagency Regional Center" that would act as a regional interagency headquarters for foreign and defense policy. This new organization would result in the unification of the Department of Defense and the Department of State (as well as other agencies and departments) at the regional level. The Interagency Regional Center (IRC) would be led by an "interagency regional director" with regional experience and expertise who would report directly to the President or Vice President of the United States. The president develops the grand strategy and establishes national security strategy, while the regional directors would implement that strategy that the regional level. The regional directors would advise and participate in the National Security Council, as requested. Regional directors would also convene to discuss cross-regional issues and activities. The IRCs would ensure long-lasting integration of all instruments of national power.

   The interagency regional director would have a military and civilian deputy. The military deputy would focus on defense issues while the civilian deputy would focus on diplomacy, development, and other critical nonmilitary issues. The civilian deputy would also act as a regional ambassador-at-large who would have coordination authority for country ambassadors and other civilian-led organizations such as Treasury, Justice, and Commerce. Country ambassadors would still formally report directly to the Secretary of State through the IRC. The civilian deputy would be in charge of coordinating all nonmilitary agencies and organizations at the regional level. During wartime, the military commander will report directly to the President through the Secretary of Defense as in the current combatant command structure, while the director and civilian deputy would focus on nation-building and post-conflict operations. During peacetime, the military would report through the IRC for engagement. For this approach to be successful, peacetime and wartime responsibilities would need to be clearly delineated and understood.

2. An intermediate approach would collocate the Department of State regional bureaus with the geographic combatant commands. These locations would be ideal to strengthen the authority of regional bureaus and allow the bureaus to operate more nimbly. Colocation of the regional assistant secretary (or alternatively, a deputy assistant secretary) in his/her staff with the geographic combatant command would allow for regional-level integration with a more unified approach and presence. Colocation of other departments and agencies, such as Central Intelligence Agency (CIA) regional offices, should also be considered.

3. An alternative intermediate approach would be for the geographic combatant command civilian deputy to act also as a regional ambassador-at-large who would have coordination authority for country ambassadors and other civilian-led organizations in the region. His/her mission under this authority would be to coordinate U.S. actions, issues, and initiatives within the region and bordering regions. The civilian deputy would have the authority to require consultation between regional organizations, but would not have the authority to compel agreement. This coordination authority would be a consultation relationship, not an authority through which chain of command would be exercised. This approach works under the current structure, but adds integration by bringing together all agencies operating within the region to coordinate regional activities.

It is critical that the United States think about how to adapt to emerging 21st century realities, both strategic and fiscal, particularly as the United State transitions from a decade of war. Long-range global trends and near-term security challenges demand a broader use of instruments of national power. The United States must take advantage of its strategic assets, and resource and restructure for a better balanced, forward-deployed approach. The Secretary of Defense, Chairman of the Joint Chiefs of Staff, the Secretary of State, and the National Security Advisor should commission a detailed follow-on study to this report to further evaluate key insights and execution of suggested recommendations.

WHOLE—OF—GOVERNMENT COORDINATION

The importance of the National Security Council (NSC) as an instrument of coordination in the foreign policy and national security direction of the Executive Branch belongs in any discussion pertaining to a possible ''Goldwater-Nichols Act ll.'' In an increasingly multipolar world, it is evident that a whole-of-government approach is needed to respond to an increasingly wider array of threats, as well as a dramatic increase in their sheer numbers. My experience in the NSC from 2009–2010 convinced me that strategic policy coordination by the NSC is its prime responsibility and is the best service it can provide the President. Gone are the days when a single department can be given the single responsibility to take on, by itself, any of the major challenges of our times. New challenges, such as cybersecurity, energy and climate security, economic security, and the rise of non-state actors indicate that the proper national interagency response spans across the traditional ''stovepiped'' menu to which we grew accustomed in the past century. Assuming that this is correct, it follows that there needs to be a ''coordinating agency'' tasked to effectuate the national security policies that require presidential decision making.

I presume that today's NSC remains afflicted by the same organizational challenges that I faced in January 2009 when I first assumed the role as National Security Advisor. The main challenges facing the NSCs of this era are resources, manpower allocation, and increasing span of activity.

One of the first decisions regarding the NSC in 2009 was to combine the NSC and Homeland Security staffs, a move that was widely applauded and which has proven itself to be extremely useful. Our security does not start or stop at our borders, and our efforts to respond to the multiple security challenges we face must be coordinated in a combined NSC staff. That task has largely been accomplished.

In 2009, as I recall, the NSC operated on an ''anemic budget'' of $4 million. In combining the two staffs, as previously discussed, it became obvious that an increase in resources was necessary. After conducting a detailed study, it was determined that $23 million was necessary to conduct the NSC's important work, which also included the funding to hire the requisite expertise to appropriately staff the NSC. This request was rejected as being out-of-line in relation to the funding of other West Wing entities. As I recall, however, we did receive an increase of $8 million, adding to the $4 million previously allocated, for a total of annual budget of $12 million. Even considering that modest increase in funding allocation, I continue to feel that the NSC has been consistently underfunded for the tasks it is asked to perform and perhaps more importantly, those that it is expected to perform.

The size of the NSC has come under criticism recently. Critics would do well to recall that in combining the Homeland Security Council (HSC) and the NSC in 2009, significant personnel efficiencies were achieved. Actually, the number of assigned personnel to the NSC is not the main problem; the main problem lies in how personnel are assigned to the NSC. The majority of personnel "detailed" to the NSC are "on temporary loan" from other government agencies. Parent agencies select the "detailees," pay their salaries, and place strict controls on how long they can be "away from home." This system causes significant personnel annual turnover rates within the NSC. As I recall, almost half of the NSC staff turned over in 2010, just one year after the administration took office. This situation exists for several reasons. One is that agencies themselves benefit from having more NSC-experienced staff, not realizing that frequent rotations impact continuity of NSC efforts. Another is that the NSC itself is not resourced to pay the salaries of the amount of personnel needed to accomplish its mission. The result of frequent personnel turnover is a detrimental effect to the experience level, efficiency, and consistency needed in the NSC itself. My view of an adequate NSC staffing composition is 3/4 "permanent personnel" and 1/4 "detailees." The length of service for "detailees" to the NSC can be easily determined by it and the respective agencies, and certainly the reforms I suggest could reduce the overall number of "detailees," which would benefit the various agencies.

My lasting conclusion with regard to the NSC's "span of activity" is that it should, first and foremost, be a very small "agency-like" organization with all the entitlements of larger agencies, such as funding for protocol, media, congressional relations, travel, etc. This is a simple resource allocation problem, but it has never been fixed. Second, the NSC should be a "policy communicating/disseminating" organization and needs to be the principal coordinating vortex for major national and international security issues. The number of Cabinet rank advisors who gather in the Situation Room to give advice to the President on the most important issues has increased significantly in the past few years. It is critical that the NSC staff be organized, resourced, and adequately staffed in order to do what is needed to coordinate interagency activities.

Lastly, the NSC should not and cannot be a policy "implementing" organization. NSC's have had a historical tendency to travel down the "slippery slope" of micromanagement as their tenure in an administration evolves. This is where the major criticism usually occurs; it is easy to lose the sense of balance between what is a primary function and what becomes an "urge" to manage the implementation of policy, something that vastly exceeds the mission of the NSC. It is, in my view, the responsibility of the National Security Advisor to create the environment that lends itself to partnerships and trust among Cabinet-rank officials who play an increasing role in the wider national security community.

In his testimony before the Committee, former Secretary of Defense Bob Gates expressed doubt about the efficacy of an interagency Goldwater-Nichols. He makes valid points that must be considered carefully. I would submit that the practical difficulties he points out underscore the important role of the of the NSC and the NSS—as a presidential instrument—can and must play a role in ensuring that decisions taken by the President and his national security team are duly and properly implemented by the interagency. I believe that the NSC's ability to help perform this essential function would be greatly advanced by the personnel and structural reforms I proposed.

Secretary Gates also testified about the Congress' vital role in setting the conditions for an efficiently run national security establishment. He noted the destructive consequences to the Department of Defense and our national security interests of perpetual partisan gridlock, budget impasses, and the recurring threat of government shutdowns. I would like to associate myself with his remarks on the need for Congress to be a part of national security reform, not only by how it funds and directs the DOD to operate, but how it conducts its legislative and oversight responsibilities.

CONCLUDING OBSERVATIONS

Mr. Chairman, Senator Reed, Members of the Committee, I thank you for allowing me to offer this testimony. I am of the opinion that the landmark legislation of Goldwater-Nichols Defense Reorganization Act of 1986, which was informed, in part, by many of the findings included in the Packard Commission Report of 1986, provided the framework for the United States Armed Forces that our country enjoys and admires today, a force that is unequalled and unrivaled anywhere. It is now time to look to the future by modernizing those areas of the legislation that are in most need of reform. Previous witnesses have provided a long and wide ranging commentary on the need for a "Goldwater-Nichols ll."

We are fortunate that many of the framers of the original legislation are still "current" on security issues, and are still providing advice to the leadership of our government and the Department of Defense. I recommend that additional use of this distinguished group be considered in any effort involving a proposed "Goldwater-Nichols ll." They are truly national assets and collectively they represent decades of unparalleled experience. It could well be that the Committee might benefit from such a group to gather once again, as they did in 1997, for the purpose of recommending the most important areas, on which there is universal agreement, for urgent reform. I hope my contribution has been useful and I look forward to helping you in any way possible in the important ongoing work of reform that serves the nation's interests.

Chairman MCCAIN. Thank you, and I thank the witnesses.

I would just add it is my understanding, General, that under Henry Kissinger, the NSC staff was 50 people. I understand now it is 400. I might argue that in the days of Kissinger, we were more successful than we are today. It is not clear to me that increasing sizes of the staffs is necessarily the answer.

I guess one of the fundamental questions I think that we are trying to confront here, that we have the COCOMs, but every time that there is a major contingency or emergency or some challenge, that we form up a joint task force, and they address it rather than the COCOMs themselves. In addition to that, obviously, we do not know the number of people on these staffs because we have never had a full accounting for not only the military personnel but the contract personnel and the civilian personnel that are all assigned to them as well. So some argue that the COCOMs should be reduced significantly in size and number because these standing task forces seem to be the vehicle for addressing the national emergencies.

I guess we can begin with you, General Jones.

Mr. JONES. Well, I think, first of all, the term 'combatant command' is one that was coined during Secretary Rumsfeld's tenure. In my view the correct title for these commands is 'unified command.' One of the reasons that AFRICOM wound up in Stuttgart, Germany was that we refused to change the title 'combatant command,' and no African leader was going to welcome a combatant command of the United States in their country. So Germany has a long history with us. They understood what we were trying to do, and they extended the invitation to put it in Stuttgart, Germany.

The overall functions of the 21st century unified command in my view are, number one, warfighting but also, number two, to by their presence, which is I think a gift of enormous value to the United States, be molded I think, as this report suggests, into a much more useful instrument of American engagement in foreign policy. I would advocate that there could be a structure where senior elements of the interagency could also be present. They would be working in the same time zone as their colleagues. It would bring a regional focus to our strategic thinking that would be extremely important. Right now in the State Department, the strategic and the operational level of involvement is located here in Washington, and as a result, we have a soda straw mentality approaching each country country by country when the world is much easier to understand if you did it by regions.

So modernizing and transforming these unified commands into a more cogent expression of our national capabilities I think makes a lot of sense and should be seriously considered for the future.

Chairman McCAIN. General Flynn?

Mr. FLYNN. Thanks, Chairman.

So I am going to be a little bit hypothetical here. You asked about sort of re-imagining. You used the word 're-imagining.' To specifically answer your question, the fighting forces inside of our combatant commands are not resourced the way you believe they are. So Army components, Marine components, naval components within a combatant command in some cases AFRICOM, parts of EUCOM—they do not exist or they do not exist in the capacity and capability to be able to actually combine themselves together with joint forces or coalition forces to do the job.

So that said, imagine only two geographic combatant commands—only two—an east and a west. You would have to have specific other commands like STRATCOM, which I believe is necessary because we do have a nuclear responsibility for this Nation for this century; Cyber Command because this is definitely a new world as I highlighted in some of the things I said. So if that is all you had, you just had an east and a west four-star that did a lot of things—they would take on a lot of things. What we have to figure out is how do we flesh out the resources, the warfighting resources, the ready capabilities that we need from all these other places that have been highlighted by the testimony that you have heard today and others and get that stuff out of the tail of the Department of Defense and get it down into the warfighting forces that we need because otherwise we are going to—you know, we have Ebola, we have some problem somewhere around the world. It is like, okay, give me some bits and pieces and we throw it together. It really has nothing to do with coming out of that combatant command.

So could you get to that? Could you get to an east and a west geographic combatant command? You know, they do not need to be services. They are headquarters. Would they be relatively large? I am not so sure if they need to be much larger than what they are doing. If you look at like a PACOM, you look at—I mean, when we talk about EUCOM, AFRICOM, CENTCOM, I mean those are interesting. Could you bring something together that commanded all those? Then what you do is you drive down the size of these headquarters, starting with the building across the river here, and the resources that they need, as well as the agencies and activities of the Department of Defense. I tell you the one that I led is way over. It is overpriced and there are too many people in it. When you look at 9/11 to the size of it today, just in that example—and I think General Jones—he nailed it when we talk about some of what these agencies and activities are doing and how bloated they are.

So could we get to that? Could we get to an east and a west? Could we drive down the number of four-stars and three-stars that we have? I mean, when I look around the world, there are not a lot of four-stars out there. There is a few when we are talking about colleagues and we talk about what exists out there. It does not mean that we get rid of every one of them, but it means that we really take a hard look and do sort of a red team analysis of what it is that I am imagining here in this hypothetical, which I actually think that it is practical. Now, could it be achieved in 4 years? It would take some time and it would certainly take a lot of effort.

Is it possible? It is possible. Can you imagine it? I can imagine it because when I look at how we fight today and how we have been fighting and how I think we will fight for at least the next 10 years, we are going to continue down this road that you have already recognized. We are stealing—so CENTCOM—I am pulling people on the battlefield. I am pulling people from PACOM, USFK, EUCOM, AFRICOM to fight a war in Iraq. From the intelligence perspective, we are pulling people from all over the place. They had no rhyme or reason to any kind of structured system that we had in place. So all those combatant commands had to pile on. It just made no sense.

It is almost like take the whiteboard, wipe it clean, and then have some effort, some analytical effort, that takes a really hard look at sort of what I would just call a team B approach to what I am addressing.

Chairman MCCAIN. Senator Reed?

Senator REED. Well, let me start with Secretary Donley. If you want to make a comment, that would be appropriate, Secretary. But there is one point in your testimony that I thought was interesting because we are going to have a huge process here of reform, and you have to start off with some tangible first steps. One step you suggested was integrating the staffs of the services. Currently the uniformed staff is there and then the civilian sector staff is here.

Can you just for a moment sort of comment on that proposal? Then I will ask General Flynn and General Jones for their perspective since they have served in different areas. Mr. Secretary, please.

Mr. DONLEY. Sir, I will turn to that just quickly in answer to Senator McCain's question about COCOMs, a couple of points real quick.

The committee's effort to redefine management headquarters and to get the Department to rebaseline all that work will be very important I think in getting a new updated baseline of the COCOM headquarters, the service component headquarters, et cetera. That is very important as you consider the way forward. That is why I focused on that area.

Second, I do think having global coverage is important across the regional combatant commands. We actually did not have global coverage until the early 2000s. We had several countries that were, quote/unquote, unassigned. So it has taken us a long time to get to the global configuration we have. You can expect changes at the margins as commanders talk about the seams and they get adjusted. But I think trying to collapse the regional structure at this point would be a step backwards.

Third point quickly on how COCOMs task organize. It makes a lot of sense to assign regional responsibilities to subunified commands or to component commanders. COCOM headquarters are not capable of doing everything themselves on their headquarters staff. One prominent example that is out there right now is the need to develop missile defense architectures. We are doing that in at least three places that I am aware of. We are doing that in the Gulf. We are doing that in Europe, including the eastern Med, and we are doing that in Asia. We need the technical expertise of the service components, air and land, to work that together, and they are doing it with allies at the operational level. So these are things that COCOM headquarters cannot do by themselves. It makes a lot of sense to task those.

On the military department headquarters, so this has a very long history. As provided for in Title 10 coming out of Goldwater-Nichols, it sort of cements these two staffs in the same headquarters. But there are functions on both sides that in some cases are almost the same function. The assistant secretaries and the services, for example, for manpower and reserve affairs, have functional responsibilities for policy and oversight that look a lot like the deputy chiefs of staff for personnel on the military side. So they are compelled to work together, but they are organizationally separated. Depending on who is assigned there, the personalities and the guidance they get from their chief or their secretary, sometimes offices such as these and these two staff do not always work well together. If you are in the field, sometimes there is confusion about where you go in the headquarters. Do you go to the secretariat for this or do you go to the deputy chief of staff for this?

Other parts of the staff that are separated actually ought to come together. Acquisition and logistics is one of those. As the committee knows, there is a long history of trying to work lifecycle management and put acquisition and logistics functions together. AT&L [the Office of the Under Secretary of Defense for Acquisition, Technology, and Logistics] does that at the OSD level, but in the services those are still separated.

So there is a lot of potential here to get to a single staff. It will be hard work, but it is I think worth doing.

Senator REED. Very quickly because my time is expiring. General Flynn, any comments? General Jones, any comments?

Mr. JONES. I do. I am sorry, Mike. Go ahead.

Mr. FLYNN. I would just say briefly having witnessed this integration between services and the department level, I think that is the right approach. I do think that there has to be more—you know, the recognition of our civilian leadership has got to be very clear. But military officers to be able to work in there because it gets into what General Jones talked about is the interagency roles. You do not have to duplicate staff. So I think that that is a good idea.

Senator REED. Thank you.

General Jones, please.

Mr. JONES. Senator, I believe that we should consider all kinds of ideas, and I think we should not probably pick any one as being the best way to do it. I think that is the value of studying things.

But just for information, the civilian-to-active duty ratios of the Department right now, with the Air Force is 1 to 1.7, civilian to military. In the Navy, it is 1 to 1.8. In the Army, it is 1 to 2.3, and in the Marine Corps, it is 1 to 8.3. So we clearly have inflated numbers in our bureaucracy both military and civilian. We need to become more efficient. We need to do things quicker. We cannot continue to take 15 years to produce a major end item, important system for the warfighter. We just have to be leaner and really reduce the size of military staffs in headquarters just across the board.

How you do the civilian secretariats and the military staff I think is something worthy of study. I do not have a clear view on how that would work. But it is certainly something we should consider.

Senator REED. Thank you very much.

Thank you, Mr. Chairman.

Chairman McCAIN. Senator Ernst?

Senator ERNST. Thank you, gentlemen, for joining us today, and thank you, Mr. Chair, for your very kind words on the floor yesterday. I certainly appreciated that.

General Flynn, I am very concerned about the military intelligence force structure and the support actually going out to the warfighter. For example, AFRICOM. Despite ISIS surging in Libya and many of the other threats on the continent, the Army has stated there is likely going to be about a 2-year delay in getting an Army theater intelligence brigade established for support in that area.

General Breedlove has also stated that in Europe the current levels of MI [military intelligence] support are very inadequate. They are lacking considering the threat that we have coming from Russia and other transnational threats and terrorism. Not much is being done to provide EUCOM with MI support.

So we have INSCOM [United States Army Intelligence and Security Command] at Fort Belvoir, Virginia, and it is this Army senior intelligence integrator. It equips, trains, and mans the Army intelligence units all around the globe. You have spent 30 years in MI. If you could please tell us in your experience if INSCOM could be better reformed to support the warfighter and how we can achieve that.

Mr. FLYNN. Okay, and this really gets to the chairman's question about what we have been talking about with combatant commands' ability to organize, to fight.

So INSCOM was a creation of the Soviet Union Cold War system that we fought at least 25 years ago now. So it is a—I am going to be very candid here. It is a bloated, almost irrelevant headquarters. We have Army component commanders underneath every geographic combatant command, actually underneath all of them. So we have an Army service component underneath EUCOM. You have one underneath CENTCOM. They are three-stars. I think in Europe it is still a four-star. But those are senior officers. The Army intelligence forces are aligned back to INSCOM. It just does not make any sense. Talk about more headquarters that you do not need.

So I think that there is a fundamental need to take a real laser focus at what you are addressing and decide whether or not INSCOM can be dissolved. You take resources and you push them out to those theater intelligence brigades which are necessary, and they function very well and they do actually work for those commanders. But the way that we have them aligned—I know the size of INSCOM's headquarters, and I honestly do not know—I cannot sit here today and tell you that I have served 5 years in combat in the last decade, and I am not sure what that particular headquarters did for me. I know what the intelligence brigades did, and I would work it through the warfighting command system.

So I think part of this reform—it is like agencies and activities and some of these other headquarters that have grown. This is one that goes back to the Cold War, and it is time to take another look at whether or not that is necessary.

Senator ERNST. That is great. Thank you for the input, General Flynn.

General Jones, in January of 2013, former Secretary of Defense Leon Panetta signed a memorandum eliminating the direct ground combat definition and assignment rule which directed the services to open the direct ground combat specialties previously closed to women by the first of January 2016 or to request an exception to policy for any direct ground combat specialties they determined should remain closed.

In your experience as the former Commandant of the Marine Corps, what would your best military advice or recommendation for the Marine Corps have been to the Secretary of Defense for 1 January? If you could expound on that please.

Mr. JONES. Well, thank you, Senator. I would like to think that my time as Commandant was one that advocated for more billets being opened for women and broader integration. I was in the Marine Corps long enough to see the separateness become one Marine Corps where we had two separate organizations for a long time and they were brought together in the 1970s I think. So I have been a staunch advocate for making as many billets as possible available to women.

The one exception that I feel strongly about is combining genders at the rifle squad, platoon, and company level simply because of the physiological differences between men and women. Overwhelmingly, that is my objection. I have served in combat as a platoon commander and a company commander in Vietnam. I have been a battalion commander. I do not see that as something that would enhance the combat warfighting capability of our units. When you look at professional sports and the National Football League, the National Hockey League, the National Basketball Association, professional tennis, professional golf, they make a distinction between men and women in terms of putting them on the same teams at the same time. I think that that analogy applies to women serving in line outfits at the very, very—at the warfighting level, as I said, at the rifle squad, platoon, and company level where I would be very careful about mandating 100 percent inclusion because I actually think that would decrease our combat capability.

Senator ERNST. Thank you. I respect your opinion very much.

Mr. JONES. Thank you.

Senator ERNST. Thank you, gentlemen.

Thank you, Mr. Chair.

Chairman McCAIN. Senator McCaskill?

Senator McCASKILL. Thank you, Mr. Chairman.

Thank you all for your service to our country and thank you for being here today.

I am going to start with you, Secretary Donley. I am aware of the pressures that have been put on the Air Force as it relates to drone operators because of the incredibly capable unit that we have in Missouri at Whiteman. I know that the Air Force is working on this problem.

But it seems to me that this is something that we did not see coming because now I have learned that the Air Force is actually considering using contractors in order to ease the burden on these drone operators.

At large, I think the issue of contractors versus active military is something that we are struggling with in our military. Certainly there is a role for contractors. Certainly we all acknowledge there is a role for contractors. Hopefully contracts that have been well scoped and competed and that are not cost-plus and that are overseen with capability and confidence as opposed to what we saw with CORS [Contracting Officer's Representatives] when I first arrived in Washington in connection with what we were spending in Iraq on particularly logistic support, LOGCAP [the Logistics Civil Augmentation Program].

So I guess my question for you, Secretary Donley, is are you comfortable that we are at a position that we are hiring contractors to do the drone work, which in fact our warfighters—the reason they are under such stress right now is because they are being asked to target and kill the enemy during the day and going home to dinner with their families. It is a new kind of warfighting. It just appears that we were not really ready to support these warfighters. I am uncomfortable that the answer is to hire civilians.

Mr. DONLEY. Senator, I cannot speak to the current state of readiness or personnel pressures on the RPA [remotely piloted aircraft] operator force, but it certainly was significant and has been for quite some time.

The demand for this capability has been off the charts, and the Air Force had discussions with Secretary Gates and his staff about what the upper limit would be. We always had difficulty. Working with my colleague, General Flynn, I remember when he was in Afghanistan. We were working these issues. The Department set targets for the Air Force to grow the number of orbits. Each time the Air Force met that goal, the goalposts were moved.

Senator McCASKILL. Right.

Mr. DONLEY. This happened two or three times in a 2- or 3-year period. So the Air Force was playing catch-up.

These aircraft take a special training, obviously, and the mission integrating these aircraft with the intelligence system and providing that instantaneous sort of sensor-to- shooter capability netted into the entire intelligence network through the DCGS [Distributed Common Ground System] has been a tremendous capability for our country. But it has also been manpower intensive, and the Air Force has been behind the power curve in doing this.

It seemed much easier and frankly the focus had been in the Congress and in the Department to just continue to buy more aircraft, which made sense. But what the Air Force was doing behind the scenes, at a time when the Air Force budget was stagnant and the Air Force was actually decreasing in size, is we had to man this force. We had to create a new job series and invent the career force for RPA operators, and we had to set up the schoolhouses. There was so much pressure on operations that it was difficult to keep up because they were also robbing from the schoolhouses.

So your point is well taken. The force has been tremendously stressed.

I am uncomfortable with having civilian contractors performing military missions. That does not sound right to me, and we need to take a close look at that interface between what is an appropriate civilian activity and what is an appropriate military activity in the sensor-to-shooter kill chain.

Senator MCCASKILL. Correct.

I am almost out of time, but I wanted to briefly, General Jones—any of you. If you want to respond to this on the record. But I am still looking for some kind of data that would support the morphing that occurred during Iraq and Afghanistan from the military with CERP [Commander's Emergency Response Program] to building highways and how we got to the point that there was a lack of accountability because it was never clear whether AID [United States Agency for International Development] was doing infrastructure and development or whether it was the active military. Obviously, there were security concerns. We had highways that probably should not ever have been built and were built under the aegis of this is fighting counterinsurgency by winning the hearts and minds, but in reality, it was probably more about our supply chain and reliability of our supply chain. This all got very murky. I have yet to see data that shows a direct relationship between the money we spent, which began with fixing the storefront broken window to the billions that were spent on vacant health centers, power plants that do not work. I could sit here and list dozens and dozens of projects.

We have got to figure this out because just because we decided using this money in fighting counterinsurgency was a good idea does not mean it necessarily was. Somebody has got to show me that it worked. I do not think anybody has been able to show that yet, and I do not want us to go down that road again until somebody produces the data that showed it had an impact.

Mr. JONES. Senator, I think that is a great question. My recollection of those days leading up to the invasion of Iraq was that the Defense Department was specifically informed that we would not do nation building. Therefore, there was no nation building plan. My recollection of the plan basically saw a military force go to Baghdad, pull down Saddam Hussein's statue, and they said, okay, we are going home. That was not the case. Everything that happened after that was very, very ad hoc and not well done. The lessons I think of that mission I think should stay with us for quite a while because I think engagement—if you are going to engage at that level in this 21st century, you need to have the operational plan to bring about the security that you need, but you also need an economic plan and you also need—if you are going to change the government, you need to make sure you have governance and rule of law in what is going to happen afterwards. The Central Command of that time did not have that plan.

Senator MCCASKILL. I want to make sure those lessons get to Leavenworth.

Mr. JONES. Exactly.

Senator MCCASKILL. Thank you.

Chairman MCCAIN. I might point out that the latest example of that is Libya, completely walking away, and many of us warned that the outcome now seems to be a new base for Al Qaeda.

Senator Ayotte, the Democrats have a gathering and if it is okay with you, I would like to recognize Senator King to go, if you do not mind. I know you do not mind.

Senator AYOTTE. Of course, absolutely.

Chairman MCCAIN. Thank you.

Senator KING. Thank you, Senator.

We are talking about supporting the warfighter. I think one of the most dramatic examples of the failure to do so and then eventually turning it around and doing so was the MRAP program.

General Jones, what have we learned from that and the fact that Secretary Gates had to move heaven and earth to make that happen? What have we learned from that experience in order to be more nimble in terms of dealing with threats on the battlefield?

Mr. JONES. Senator, this is one of the largest problems that we have in the current construct of the Defense Department. I might even say that even presidential directives are ignored. I will give you an example of a meeting between the President of Algeria, President Bouteflika, and President Bush in which the President of Algeria asked the American President for night vision goggles for his air force, pretty standard stuff. The President said let us do that, and he said we will do that. To this day, the Algerian air force have never received them. It is simply because in the bureaucracy that we built, there are too many people that can say no and too many areas in which it can be blocked. I can give you chapter and verse of other examples in dealing with foreign countries who really want to have a relationship with the United States and really want to buy United States products and eventually just throw up their hands and go buy French or Israeli or another country simply because it is just too hard and too slow. As I said, there are examples of presidential directives being consumed by the bureaucracy and its inertia.

Senator KING. But we have got to try to figure this out because lives are at stake. American lives are at stake if we cannot do an MRAP, if takes 2 years instead of 2 months, and there was a clear need. Not necessarily in this setting but perhaps following up in writing, you could give us some suggestions about how to deal with this bureaucratic issue. There has got to be some kind of expedited path. Are lives at stake? Yes. Then it goes in a different direction.

Mr. JONES. Absolutely. But my opinion is you have got to reduce the bureaucracy. There are simply too many people that can say no and too many people that can block it. If we cannot do it for our own troops, let alone the troops of our allies and our friends, we are at risk I think in terms of, as you said, Senator, costing more lives because of our inefficiency. That is something that I think Goldwater-Nichols II could really take a look at and trim the bureaucracy so that there are fewer people who can say no.

Senator KING. It seems to me we have parallel bureaucracies now. We have the Secretary of Defense with all that that entails, and then we have the Joint Staff. We have got sort of two very large entities. Would that be where you would start?

Mr. JONES. I think those are two very large bureaucracies. I noticed on the Secretary of Defense's staff, we have 70 flag and general officers. On the Secretary of Defense staff, 70 flag and general officers working today. So this is enormous and contributes to the inversion that we have created with huge headquarters and their survival, and the amount of resource they consumes comes at the direct expense of the fighting forces, our fighting capabilities.

Mr. FLYNN. If I can just make one quick comment.

Senator KING. Yes, Secretary Donley, please.

Mr. FLYNN. In my last deployment, I spent almost 18 months in Afghanistan. The first office that I went back to the Pentagon and thanked—I purposely did this—was the Rapid Fielding Office, which was a creation of the inertia that was required on the battle-field because just literally the dozens of urgent need statements that were coming from the battlefield. So this rapid needs office was stood up, a bunch of really great Americans, and they were rapidly turning as fast as they could those kinds of things. The Secretary, both Rumsfeld and Gates, really turned it on. They were able to move things faster. But even then, they had to work around all this mess that we have all highlighted here. I just think that we have got to figure out how we can speed up the process when we go to war. We have to.

I will leave one other comment. Secretary Rumsfeld came out to visit us in Balad, Iraq early as in the 2004 time frame. I will never forget the conversation. A small group. We told him. We told him if you told us that we were going to go to war and we were not going to come home until we won, we would fight this war differently. But when you tell me that I am on a 9-month deployment, I am on a 6-month deployment, I am on a year deployment, what you have just told is I am going to participate in this conflict. I am going to return forever. If you told me, Flynn—and we were looking right at him. If you told me, Flynn, you are not going to come home until we win, how would you fight this war differently. Trust me, Senator. We would have fought it differently, much differently.

Senator KING. Well, I appreciate this.

Mr. Chairman, I think this is one of the areas we really have to look at, the whole issue of bureaucracy because it is one thing how long it takes to get socks through the process, but if we are talking about an MRAP or ammunition or lifesaving equipment and we are in a battle space that is changing so fast that you just cannot fight the last war. So I hope you fellows can help us think this through because the tendency of any bureaucracy—and these are not bad people, by the way, but the tendency of any bureaucracy is, A, to say no and, B, to grow. I think it is something we are going to have to—this is the purpose of these hearings is to help us to address these questions. But this puts a very fine point on the necessity, it seems to me.

Thank you very much, gentlemen.

Thank you, Mr. Chairman.

Chairman MCCAIN. 70 flag and general officers that work for the Secretary of Defense?

Mr. JONES. That is correct.

Senator KING. I wonder how many there were in all of World War II.

Chairman MCCAIN. There was a PACCOM [Pacific Ocean Areas Command] and there was a European Command.

Senator Ayotte?

Senator AYOTTE. Thank you, Chairman.

I want to thank all of you for your distinguished records of service to the country.

General Flynn, I wanted to ask—really have all of you comment on something—your comments where you said I have also served many years in combat and have suffered from the lack of many capabilities we needed to fight our enemies and found myself fighting the Pentagon is much more than our enemies.

The one thing that I have noticed in my first term in the Senate here is that when we get feedback from the ground and we get feedback from the soldiers, the airmen, the sailors, and they tell us about something, it becomes almost retributive in terms of when they are telling us something and what happens to them to give us the honest opinion of what they need from the ground and what they think. I feel like I have a responsibility to get that opinion, not just to hear from the service chief but to hear from the people who are really affected. The experience that I have seen around here is that, listen, you got to do it secretly. You got to do it quietly, and if they find you out, they will root you out.

So how do we change that culture? You know there is a law that says if a Member of Congress—you legally can talk to a Member of Congress about your opinion. So how do we change that cultural problem that seems to be, in my view, something that I have been shocked by.

Mr. FLYNN. I could spend all day, and I will try to be very, very brief. I once wrote and sent in an urgent needs statement because we were actually using the equipment. So it was an off-the-shelf buy that we did and we are using it and it is working. Our operational guys going and doing raids in houses were using it. We pieced it together, and we said, okay, this is something that we want to go to our larger joint task force. So I wrote it, sent it up through the channels. I did all my back channel stuff to all my buddies because we were trying to move at a different speed. When it made it through the system, it got into the Army, in this case—but not always the Army is the bad guy. Folks on the Army staff said that is not what they need. He does not need that. Who does he think he is?

Now, at the time, I was a colonel. These senior guys come out and they say, Flynn, if one of you ever need anything, call me. So I called up the boss, in this case the Deputy Secretary of Defense. I was calling from combat. So they took the call. Good enough, the

DepSecDef said let me look into it and we were able to get the capability.

Now, that is about as bold as you can get because you know what? I was, in this case, in Iraq and I was like, okay, what the hell are they going to do. We need this capability. I am finding a system that just could not, did not respond.

Senator AYOTTE. What worries me is that you were able to do that. I can assure you that that has happened, and the person who tried to do that in your shoes, instead of getting what they need, got punished in some way. That is what worries me. Am I wrong about this?

Mr. FLYNN. No. I think you are right. I see it right now. I actually see it happening right now because I have a lot of friends that are still serving, especially in the intelligence community where they feel so—it is not just about this assessment stuff. It is actually about other things that are going on, and it is like they feel encumbered, limited, constrained to say something because particularly with systems, there is some equipment out there that is just flat not working.

We are getting ready to send some more forces to combat here. The Secretary of Defense was in here the other day talking to you about it. I know down at the troop level because I see it, they are asking for a particular piece of equipment and their headquarters are saying do not ask for that piece of equipment. In fact, in one case, one headquarters has said I do not want to see any more urgent needs coming through this headquarters. Now, for a commander to say that, it is—I guess I am not surprised, Senator, but——

Senator AYOTTE. What can we do to empower that, I mean, to empower that people can speak freely? What more can we do?

Mr. JONES. I think it is, first and foremost, a leadership problem, and I think service chiefs owe it to put out guidance to their forces that this is our system. This is what happens. You are going to be—in the course of your career, you are going to talk to Members of Congress. You are going to talk to staff. The only thing we would ask is that what you tell them you have told us so that everybody is on the same sheet of music. You do not, on the one hand, keep your mouth shut while you are talking to your commander and then unload on your commander behind closed doors.

So I think that we can do a lot more in the leadership department to try to educate our men and women in uniform exactly why this is part of the system. The other thing is positive leadership means that you do not take retribution out on people for speaking honestly about what they feel. So I think there is a way to do it. I just think it takes more focus and it takes positive leadership and guidance to make sure that people in the respective service understand that this is the policy. That still will not stamp it out, but it will help.

Mr. DONLEY. I would associate myself 100 percent with General Jones' remarks. This is a leadership issue. As Members of Congress, I encourage you to keep those channels open and exercise your prerogative to talk to anybody you feel you need to talk to, to mix it up with our men and women in uniform.

At the same time, as a service leader, we tell our forces, our civilians, our military personnel, use the chain of command. I would ask if something gets into a congressional channel, I am asking why is it not coming to me or the chief. Why is it not coming up through the leadership channels? So it is a leadership issue, and we should be encouraging our people to be straight with their chain of command and with anybody who asks from the outside.

Senator AYOTTE. So I appreciate all your comments on this. I think people would be straight with their chain of command if they felt that they were not going to get punished for doing so. So that is my big concern.

Mr. JONES. Senator, I think you probably had this experience as well too that in units that are well led, you do not have that problem.

Senator AYOTTE. Right.

Mr. JONES. Units that demonstrate that trait, that negative trait, are generally led by people who are somewhat insecure and cannot tolerate that just psychologically.

Senator AYOTTE. Right, because the leader will take feedback of all forms and be able to address it.

Mr. JONES. You can overcome that.

Senator Ayotte [presiding]: Thank you.

It looks like I am here. So I am going to call on Senator Sullivan.

Senator SULLIVAN. Well, I appreciate everybody's testimony and again your service, gentlemen.

I want to dig in again. I think you might be seeing here maybe a little bit of consensus on the committee on the issue. General Jones, you wrote about it very articulately in your testimony, and all of you have been speaking to it on the tooth-to-tail ratio issue.

I know this is a big question, but why do you think it has exploded so much? Is it just the normal kind of desire of bureaucracies to always grow whether it is at DOD or NATO [North Atlantic Treaty Organization] or the EPA [Environmental Protection Agency]? I mean, why do you think it exploded? Because I think that can help us get to some of the answers.

Then on this issue of just 77 flag officers, do you think it would make sense for us, as opposed to try and reposition each flag officer position, say, in the Secretary's Office, to just pass a law saying, hey, you will have no more than 25 flag officers. You figure out what they should be doing?

Why do you think it has grown, and then how do you think we can get a handle on it?

I will ask one final question. General Milley has been really focusing on this issue because the Army has been required to undertake a lot of cutbacks, at least for now. I think he is looking at the wisdom of these cutbacks and to what degree the tooth-to-tail ratio is out of whack. What advice would you give him, who is really real-time struggling with this issue? But I think it is an important one that you could see some consensus building here in the committee. I know I threw a lot at you, but feel free to, any of you, take a crack at any of those questions. Thank you.

Mr. DONLEY. Senator, I will take a first cut at it. First of all, I think it is the nature of bureaucracies to grow over time. So this issue of regularly addressing the need for greater efficiencies is an extremely important one. DOD's bureaucracy is no different than any other. It needs to be pruned.

Senator SULLIVAN. Do you think we are only entity that can really do that effectively?

Mr. DONLEY. I think Congress has a very strong role to play because this is your role to oversee the Department in this kind of a context.

I do think Congress has effective tools that it can use. At times in the past, Congress has put ceilings on headquarters activities in the Department down to the service level, and the Congress currently has limits on general officers at each grade. So you do have toolsavailable.

The one aspect that I would ask you to think about—and it is a little bit new from our decades' old experience—is the rise of the contractor workforce. I think the Department needs to get a handle on that and is in the process of doing that and trying to figure out how many contractors are supporting its headquarters activities. So the way I advised Secretary Hagel on this, when we did the OSD review a couple of years ago—you will recall that he had given direction for 20 percent reductions in all management headquarters in the Department, including OSD.

Senator SULLIVAN. Did that happen? You hear that everybody does that. The bureaucracies grow. So it does not look like it always works.

Mr. DONLEY. No. I think it is underway, and it has been underway for a couple of years. Secretary Gates started this in his efficiencies work in 2011. It got reinforced by Secretary Hagel. Now it is getting reinforced again by Congress. Actually one of the complexities the Department is going through now is to how to unite all those efficiencies that had been set in motion that are now piled on each other sort of in three different time frames over the last 3 or 4 years. So I think the work is underway, and what the committee has directed the Department to do in this management headquarters review will help set a new baseline for that.

But getting back to the contractors, you have to not just control the authorizations, but you have to control the money because if you allow the headquarters to have more money to work with, then they will buy contractor support with those resources. So getting a handle on how many contractors are supporting the headquarters and in what contexts is an important part of reestablishing a good baseline over these headquarters activities.

Senator SULLIVAN. General Jones, General Flynn, any comments?

Mr. FLYNN. Just really quick because I am not sure you were here, Senator, when General Jones talked about civilian-to-military ratios.

Senator SULLIVAN. No. I did hear that.

Mr. FLYNN. Of everything I have heard today, that is a really, really important set of data to really hone in on and take a look at because it addresses a bigger issue than what you are talking about. So when we are really looking at reform, I think that is super important.

The other is the flag officer ratio within the military. If you look at historical ratios, you know, how many flag officers per how many troops, as far back in time as you want to go, I would recommend that you go take a look at that because we actually have more flag officers per fighting unit than we did when we were doing really, really big things. So it is worth taking a look at as part of this effort.

Mr. JONES. I do not have the figures, but I do have the active duty-to-enlisted ratios in the militaries. In the Air Force, it is 1 officer for every 4.1 enlisted. In the Navy, it is 1 officer for every 4.9; in the Army, 1 officer for 4.1; and in the Marine Corps, 1 officer for every 7.8 enlisted. That is the officer-to-enlisted ratios. That has been fairly consistent over time.

With regard to your question about how do we get here, I completely agree with my colleagues. As a matter of fact, I noticed, when I was in the Pentagon, that everybody is for change as long as the change is done to somebody else. That is just the inherent personality of a bureaucracy. I believe honestly to enact the kind of change that we critically need here, it is going to take an external effort. I do not mean this pejoratively or critically of my former colleagues in the Pentagon. They are working like crazy trying to keep up with this very difficult world. But it is going to take an outside—and they should participate in it, but it is going to take a focused, separate outside organization much like the Defense Reform Task Force of 1997 to really think this through and how to do it.

Senator SULLIVAN. Thank you, gentlemen.

Thank you, Madam Chair.

Senator AYOTTE. Thank you.

General Jones, it sounds like you are signing up for duty—I like that—with this outside task force.

So since the chairman left me to close out this hearing, I cannot help myself since I have such a great panel here of incredible experts on national security issues. I have to ask you about something that has just been developing, which is yesterday the IAEA [International Atomic Energy Agency] issued its report on the prior military dimensions of Iran's nuclear program. Have you had a chance to take a look at that?

One of the pieces of it talks about the fact we know that Iran—we have had serious concerns about the Parchin facility and what they have done there in terms of conducting experiments related to the design of the core of a nuclear bomb. We also know that they took activities even during the negotiations process to demolish and change things at that facility.

So the IAEA report—one of the pieces of it concerns me because the IAEA concluded that the extensive activities undertaken by Iran at that facility since February of 2012 have seriously undermined the agency's ability to conduct effective verification.

So I just wanted to ask you sort of post-agreement here—the IAEA report issued yesterday. So I am not going to ask you to render an opinion on it. You have not seen it yet. But I think it raises some verification concerns. We had the testing of the long-range missile in October, which I have not seen a response yet from our administration on, that is in violation of existing U.N. [United Nations] resolutions, and many of us have long been concerned about their missile program because you do not need an

ICBM [intercontinental ballistic missile] unless you are interested in delivering a nuclear weapon to the United States.

So I just wanted to get your opinions, especially General Flynn and Jones, on where we are with Iran and where we are post-agreement, if you have concerns, what they are and what we should be doing.

Mr. JONES. I have just spent some time in the Gulf region talking to various leaders of our friends and allies. The word that most came up in conversations is the word 'existential threat.' Most of our friends and allies in the Gulf, quite apart from the agreement that was reached with Iran, still consider Iran to be an existential threat for the foreseeable future. As a matter of fact, one of the leaders said this agreement may paper over our concerns for a few years, but make no mistake about it. We are going to be fighting Iran for 25 years or 30 years. This is not going away.

So I think time will tell whether Iran is going to be trusted. My personal view is they are not going to be.

Senator AYOTTE. I think even just even in the immediate aftermath of the agreement——

Mr. JONES. You would think.

Senator AYOTTE.—things are not going exactly how you would think they would.

Mr. JONES. Yes. You would think.

But we entered into this agreement not just in isolation but with our P5 Plus 1 partners, and they are bright people, intelligent, and trying to do the right thing.

But I just think Iran has yet to prove itself that it is ready to join the family of nations in the way of doing trade, in the way of normalized relations, and do not worry about Hezbollah, do not worry about Hamas, do not worry about the fact that they are supporting a war in Yemen, and all the other things that they are doing. So until there is really a behavioral change at the leadership level in Iran, we should be very, very careful about what we buy into with them. I have seen no evidence that they are trustworthy.

Chairman McCain [presiding]: I thank the witnesses and I thank you for your service, and I thank you for helping us in this very significantly difficult challenge. The more we talk, the greater the challenge becomes. So I thank you. It has been extremely helpful, and we will be calling on you in the future. Thank you.

This hearing is adjourned.

[Whereupon, at 11:30 a.m., the hearing was adjourned.]